ARMS AND THE MAN

A Study of Select American War Novelists

Manisha Mathur

ATLANTIC

PUBLISHERS & DISTRIBUTORS (P) LTD

Published by

ATLANTIC

PUBLISHERS & DISTRIBUTORS (P) LTD

7/22, Ansari Road, Darya Ganj,
New Delhi-110002
Phones : +91-11-40775252, 23273880, 23275880, 23280451
Fax : +91-11-23285873
Web : www.atlanticbooks.com
E-mail : orders@atlanticbooks.com

Branch Office
5, Nallathambi Street, Wallajah Road,
Chennai-600002
Phones : +91-44-64611085, 32413319
E-mail : chennai@atlanticbooks.com

ISBN 978-81-269-1724-2

Printed in India at Glorious Printers, A-13, D.S.I.D.C.,
Jhilmil Industrial Area, Delhi-110095

Preface

Warfare has been incessant in human history since times immemorial and there have been innumerable reasons behind every conflict and aggression. For instance, the Trojan War was fought for Helen of Troy, the most beautiful woman on Earth, while the Mahabharata was a war for the triumph of 'dharma' or the victory of right over wrong. In recent times, the First World War was prompted by a desire of colonial expansion, while the Second World War was an outcome of Hitler's policy of aggrandizement.

Literature and history are inextricably linked. Every historical event has an impact on literature as history has inspired many works of fiction and poetry. The French Revolution inspired Dickens to write his classic work *A Tale of Two Cities*, while President Abraham Lincoln's death motivated the poet Walt Whitman to compose his famous elegy 'While Lilacs Last in Dooryard Bloom'd'.

As a student of history and literature, I have always wanted to study the impact of war (especially Second World War) on literature and examine how writers of fiction have reacted towards combat. American fiction aroused my interest because the American war novelist has consistently exposed the true nature of war, dispelling visions of glory from combat. Writers like Stephen Crane, Thomas Boyd, Dos Passos and Ernest Hemingway have effectively portrayed the horror and revulsion of war in their novels. The novelists who are the focus of attention in this study, viz. James Jones, Norman Mailer, Irwin Shaw, Joseph Heller and Kurt Vonnegut used their experience as combatants in the Second World War to debunk combat and strongly castigate the absurdity and lunacy of war.

What is most intriguing about these novelists is the fact that they do not merely depict the glory of battle scenes in their novels but move beyond the grisly and grimy Islands of the Pacific (where Americans were fighting the Japanese) to address broader issues like the regimentation of the army and the political, social, moral and psychological implications of war. The novelists express the hope that through their novels they would be able to sensitize the future generations about the futility and meaninglessness of war.

The book will be useful for the students and teachers of American literature. Besides, it will prove immensely beneficial to those doing research in American literature and/or authors who deal with war in their works.

Manisha Mathur

Acknowledgements

I express my heartfelt gratitude towards my teacher and mentor, Professor Madhu Mehrotra, who guided me at every step. But for her encouragement, able assistance, painstaking efforts and erudite contribution, I would not have been able to complete this project successfully. She has been a source of strength and support to me all these years and whatever results I have been able to achieve are entirely due to her blessings.

I would like to thank my husband, Sanjiv for his unqualified and strong support and encouragement. He has been my anchor and even though this was not his subject, he provided valuable inputs that helped me tremendously. I would also like to thank my children Acriti and Utcarsh who never complained about my busy schedule and supported me throughout my endeavour. I extend my gratitude towards my wonderful and loving inlaws, Prof. L.N. Mathur and Mrs. Manju Mathur, who have always encouraged me in my endeavours. My parents, Mr. R.S. Mathur, Mrs. Shashi Mathur and my sister, Tina, have been a source of strength and sustenance and I thank them profusely. I would like to thank my dear friend, Manpreet, who gave me the much needed push and prevailed upon me to get this work published. I express my gratitude towards the Indo-American Studies Centre (IASC), Hyderabad and New Delhi for providing me excellent library facilities.

Manisha Mathur

Contents

Introduction

1

The Second World War left behind a legacy of hatred and destruction and gave us the most powerful weapon that had the potential to destroy mankind itself—the terrible, man-made Frankenstein monster, the atomic bomb and its deadlier nuclear version, which threatens to obliterate the world today. It transformed United States of America into a superpower, because it was the U.S.A., which developed and used the atomic bomb against Japan. The seeds of the Second World War were sown in the post-World War I era itself. Germany was crushed, humbled, defeated and wanted to fight back. This country fought the Second War in order to reverse the verdict of the First and destroy the settlement which followed it. The settlement in question was the Treaty of Versailles signed after the First Great War was over and which sought to annihilate Germany completely. On May 7, 1919, the draft of a treaty was presented to a delegate, summoned from Germany. His immediate objection and Germany's subsequent protests had very little effect, and on June 28, in the Hall of Mirrors in the Chateau de Versailles, the treaty was signed. Ratified by Germany on July 9, it came into force on January 10, 1920. The seeds of trouble for the next twenty years were sown in those articles of the treaty that Germany had the most obvious grounds for resenting, whether as offensive to its national honour or as unduly oppressive and vindictive. The treaty stipulated that Germany must pay huge war indemnities or reparations to the Allied powers. The word 'reparations' hung like a shadow over Europe and it was seen as an undertaking to make good the war losses of the Allies. The amount of reparations to be exacted from Germany was assessed at one hundred and thirty-two billion gold marks.

Most historians are of the opinion that the war could have been avoided, but the two decades that have come to be known as the interwar years, were years of lost opportunities, opportunities that could have avoided the conflagration that erupted only two decades after the First War was over. There was so much optimism in the post World War I decade of 1920s that was harshly dispelled by the crashes and crises of the 1930s, so many hopes of peace and prosperity that were dashed by the collapse of the New World hastily constructed after 1918, that the chain of events suggested a sort of political battle between the forces of good and evil which culminated in yet another orgy of death and destruction. A situation emerged after the First World War that greatly endangered stability and led to disruption instead of cohesion, as opportunities for unification were defeated and weakening tendencies leading towards disruption became rampant. The Second World War, was a mammoth conflict that claimed the lives of seventeen million military personnel while civilian deaths were even greater as a result of starvation, bombing raids, massacres, epidemics and other war related causes. The war began on September 1, 1939 when Germany invaded Poland and Hitler resolved to create a Third Reich larger than the Empire of Charlemagne and more powerful than the empire of Napoleon. The Pacific War began in 1941, with the Japanese attack on Pearl Harbour. Virtually all countries that had participated in World War I were involved in the Second World War as well. Many historians consider World War II to be the only true World War due to the overwhelming number of nations involved and the extraordinary number of theatres—from Europe and the Soviet Union to North Africa, and from China and South East Asia to the Pacific. In World War I non-European theatres had seen quick and short colonial battles, but in World War II these theatres demanded far more resources and human sacrifice.

Warfare has been a major literary theme, going as far back as Homer's epic *The Iliad*. War has been a compelling subject in

American Literature and could be found in the Leatherstocking novels of James Fennimore Cooper and still remains a popular subject as is evident from the scores of novels that have been written about the Iraq War in the twenty-first century. War has always been a powerful theme in American fiction from the time that Stephen Crane wrote *The Red Badge of Courage* his epic novel about the Civil War. Crane's hero Henry Fleming shows a lot of optimism about the war. In contrast to the twentieth-century tradition that questions war and the modern world, many American war novels combine a celebration of patriotism and bravery with a lament over the pain and suffering that necessarily accompanies warfare. These patriotic novelists do not question the notions of honour and glory and see war as a noble endeavour and the battlefield as an arena in which a man can establish his Manhood.

Patrick Paul Christie believes that the release of Steven Spielberg's World War II epic *Saving Private Ryan* was a major cultural event of the summer of 1998. Christie is of the opinion that Spielberg's film was a revelation to many Americans whose knowledge of the Second World War was limited to the 'sanitized portrayals' found in the plethora of B grade films of the 1940s and '50s. *Saving Private Ryan*, with the full weight of Hollywood's technological magic behind it, graphically portrays the horror and bloodshed of the Normandy Landings and the bitter fighting of the days and weeks that followed. The audience watches aghast as a wounded man is dragged ashore by a comrade who ducks an explosion and then resumes dragging his 'buddy'. The camera pulls back, and we see that the wounded man now has no body below his waist. Equally gruesome images that show the capricious nature of war surround this incident. For example, a soldier has his helmet dented by a bullet. He removes it to look at the dent in wonder and seconds later receives a bullet in the middle of the forehead.

The film's main plot revolves around the search for Private Ryan whose brothers have already been killed in combat, and the plan is to preserve his life by sending him home but ironically, in order to find him the lives of eight other soldiers are put in jeopardy. In the midst of war's horrors, Spielberg explores the value of the individual and the paradoxical place of the human being in a society at war. The main character, Captain Miller, attempting to explain why he follows orders that endanger himself and his patrol, declares that he is simply trying to 'earn me the right' to go home. For Miller, the individual must be subordinate to the needs of society as a whole, even to the extent of sacrificing his life. Spielberg's film presents its audience with a vision of war as absurd and brutal. This vision has its origins in muddy battlefields where mass slaughter of human beings took place. *Saving Private Ryan* is rooted in a literary tradition that began with many of the novels that were published in the aftermath of the First Great War and that continue to be found in print even today. In these novels authors use modern technological wars as settings in which to work out their concerns about the plight of the individual caught up in and beleaguered by twentieth-century industrial culture. As Paul Fussell argues: "Beginning with World War I, authors have used the battlefield experience to stand as a virtual allegory of political and social cognition in our time. The soldier becomes a twentieth-century Everyman, and the battlefield an allegorical representation of the world we inherit" (Fusell, 26). Spielberg's film debunks war in a forceful manner. His characters are certainly brave, but their bravery falls short of being ennobling. Captain Miller's bravery, for example, earns him an uncontrollable shaking of the hand that embarrasses both himself and his troops.

The present work centers upon select post World War II novelists who debunk combat and look upon warfare as ridiculous and life negating. Malcolm Cowley observes that the novels about World War II are wide ranging in subject and content when compared to novels about World War I. The novelists of the First war focus on brutal hand-to-hand combat, war in trenches and maiming and killing of soldiers on the battlefield. However, novelists of the Second World War not only focus on combat in the jungles of Philippines and the battlegrounds of Europe but also address larger issues pertaining to war, as their canvas is extremely broad. They debunk combat not only because it is life negating, causes violence, bloodshed and immense suffering of the soldier but also focus on the latent dangers and long-term impact of war. These novelists move beyond depicting military tactics and strategies of fighting to tackle broader issues like totalitarianism of the army, dehumanization of soldiers who are a part of this institution, the political implications of war, the criticism of the capitalistic society and the American greed which dragged the country into conflict, the despair and fear of soldiers fighting the war and the impact of war on the civilian population of a country.

The focus of attention is five novelists viz. Norman Mailer, James Jones, Irwin Shaw, Joseph Heller and Kurt Vonnegut. Each of these writers had participated in the war and encountered its numerous horrors. There is a persistent note of despair, disillusionment, and rebellion, spiritual and moral collapse in the novels of these writers. The novels depict men attempting to 'seize the day' before death erases them, or struggling to articulate their own principles in a battle to retain rational integrity before the irrationality of death. The war novel, harshly castigating combat and severely criticizing the senseless violence caused during combat developed as a specific genre in the 1940s and novels about the Second World War were written even during the 1950s and 1960s. This type of novel therefore became a very important part of American fiction.

American Literature especially American fiction underwent a transformation in the post World War II period and the reasons for the development of the war novel were deeply rooted in the social, political and cultural changes that took place after the war. The 1940s were a unique literary period. The demise of an earlier generation of major writers took place during this phase, albeit metaphorically. The literary and political wars of the 1930s came to an end and the Second World War acted as a watershed as it had a major impact on the psyche of the new writers. The horrors of the atomic bomb, the Holocaust and the immense destruction caused by the war itself gave birth to new ideas, techniques and ideologies. Existentialism as a theory filtered into America and new themes were introduced in American fiction. Writers turned to techniques like Black Humour, Absurdist fantasies and satire.

To begin with, larger cultural shifts gave birth to a new literary endeavour. The changes brought about by the Second World War put considerable pressure on writers, older ones as well as the younger, but especially on the newer generation, (many of whom had served in the war) to evolve a new style of writing. The war and its tremendous impact made it incumbent upon the serious novelist to rethink purely traditional forms and ideas. The novelist, moving on a large scale, even if sympathetic towards writers like Hemingway and Faulkner, as writers like Mailer were, had to respond to new themes, new tensions, new attitudes and ways of expressing them through new modalities and textures. The change had to be made otherwise the new writer would not be taken seriously.

The situation was made complicated because of the presence of the earlier generation of major writers well after the war's end. Hemingway was alive and writing. Faulkner's *A Fable*, an ambitious work about the war was not a symbol of decline and this novel was about to be written, proving that Faulkner was still a force to be reckoned with in the literary world. Older writers like Steinbeck, Richard Wright and O' Hara were working prolifically and while Fitzgerald was dead his work spilled over into the decade. The presence of older writers acted as a sluggish influence on the novel. However, different cultural circumstances of the post war world demanded new beginnings. It is interesting to note what James Baldwin was to say later of his relationship to Richard Wright, that the sons had to kill the fathers to free themselves was true of an entire generation. Beloved as Hemingway, Fitzgerald and Faulkner were to those growing up on American fiction, these old masters had to be put behind, and the old order had to change yielding place to the new. Walter B. Rideout says about the war: "One of the effects of modern war is to alienate us from the recent past. In our consciousness war develops like a trauma between 'after' and 'before', until it is sometimes hard to believe that 'before' was a part of us at all" (Rideout, 89).

The war had indeed changed everything. The world before the war was very different from the world 'after' the war. Politically and economically the war was a blessing in disguise for the American people as it brought an end to the Great Depression. The war stimulated the economy in ways that Roosevelt's pre-war measures could not, leading to many accusations that Roosevelt created the war in order to end the Depression. Revisionist historians believe that America's entry into the War was primarily due to the President's efforts as after he assumed office in 1940, he decided to provide aid to Britain, in order to assist the country in its war efforts. It was decided that arms and ammunition for Britain's war effort would be provided by American industries. The President proposed the lend-lease program, which authorized him to supply aid to Britain on the condition that after the war they would return in kind the guns and ships loaned to them. Although Congressional approval and White House implementation of lend-lease made the United States all but a belligerent in fighting, it proved insufficient to bring the nation directly into war. Throughout 1941, according to Revisionists, Roosevelt was trying to find a rationale for entering into the conflict.

After the Nazi attack on Soviet Union in June and incidents in the North Atlantic between German submarines and two American ships, Roosevelt ordered the Navy to escort convoys of American and Allied ships and to shoot German and Italian warships on sight. Despite the existence of an undeclared naval war between Germany and the United States the President hesitated to ask for a formal declaration of war because most of the American public still favoured neutrality. At this juncture according to the Revisionist historians, Roosevelt believed he could obtain a public consensus in favour of war only if the country were attacked by a foreign power. The Revisionists believe that he allegedly created this consensus by provoking the Japanese into the attack on Pearl Harbour by introducing embargos on scrap metals and petroleum products that Japan needed for its war machine and thereby increasing tension between Japan and the United States. When Japan attacked the Pearl Harbour, American entry into the war was official. Once the war began, the economy leaped ahead with such momentum that every aspect of the system benefited. While the European economy suffered due to the war, American economy progressed.

The war transformed America into a world power. Nuclear power was theirs alone and even when the Soviet Union joined, the American technology seemed invincible and far superior. Food surpluses not deficiencies became a feature of the economy as the Americans had problems in storing their grain in the 1950s while the rest of the world, devastated by the war reached the brink of starvation. The average American ate enough each day compared to two Europeans or three Orientals. In many sectors such as oil, steel, electricity and industrial equipment the United States attained the highest position. The buying power of the average American exceeded that of the rest of the worlds by fifteen hundred percent. Poverty areas as many economists observed existed, but were 'silent and hidden.' The average poor white and Southern black was still economically better off than almost all the rest of the foreign population and the silent and hidden poor population of America still fared better than the rest of the world. This was the situation 'after' 1945. America was a world power, a super hero and a country that had forced the stubborn Japanese into surrender by dropping the atomic bomb on Hiroshima and Nagasaki. This was the America lauded and praised by tne popular press and magazines of the post-war world.

The novelists and especially those who wanted to write about the war did not see these positive aspects of America. The war had boosted the down in the dumps economy but writers like Norman Mailer, Joseph Heller and Kurt Vonnegut who had participated in this great conflict were disgusted by the war. Memories of violence, the bestiality of the Holocaust and the brutality of Hiroshima were firmly etched in their mind. For them, especially writers like Mailer, American prosperity meant materialism, which was negative and retrograde. Mailer who had Leftist leanings wrote *The Naked and the Dead* as a war novel with a strong undercurrent of social protest. The army is not the only dehumanizing force in the novel and there are strong nuances of anger at social attitudes, which transform human values into mob values. Mailer strongly believes that it is excessive materialism that made America participate in the war. The war was created by America's social attitude. There is much in the novel to substantiate Dos Passos's view of America being poisoned by the Big Money, the antidote for which was a return to Jeffersonian democracy.

Destruction continued throughout the 1950s and 1960s first with the Korean War and then with Vietnam War. Science and technology, which was a yardstick for measuring progress, seemed vicious and not heroic to these writers. There is a lot of cynicism among the writers of this period who questioned the very idea of existence. Thus the novelists of the period continuously talk about the shattering of the American Dream, which was in fact a refrain from the 1920s and the 1930s. By far the largest part of war literature comes under the rubric of alienation and estrangement from the dominant culture and disaffection sometimes from self and nature. The fictional hero is an 'outsider' who feels that he does not belong.

These novelists were forsaking social commitment to seek personal publicity and were pursuing outlandish themes as a means of locating themselves outside a bourgeoisie framework of reference. Individualism had become important in American fiction. This too was on offshoot of the belief that prevailed after the war that survival had become important and each individual had to survive in the 'crazy world' shown in Heller's *Catch 22*. Self therefore became extremely important and an intense personal note entered American war fiction. An article in the *Life* magazine of 1955, chastised the novelists for not showing America as it really was, the land of plenty and prosperity where each person could pursue his or her dream. The novelists of the era stubbornly refused to sell this idea to the rest of the world. The adversary novel was born as the novelist refused to project the 'official' version of America's success story.

Frederick Karl is of the opinion that this tendency was present even in the America of 1850s when Hawthorne wrote his adversary fictions. This was a period of tremendous activity, as the years preceding the Civil War were full of political maneuvering, polemics, economic expansion, growth of railroads and considerable migration. Yet Hawthorne moved outside this aspect to 'marginal discontinuous' area. Poe sought his vision of

America in aspects of English Gothic, in tales of horror and nightmare, an unrecognizable America. Melville moved his protagonists to sea, in order to remove them from an America that apparently was a source of confusion to him. There on the sea, the protagonists made their decision, of salvation or doom, free of any close attachments to the country. The American writers therefore have always moved quite explicitly outside any official version of American life and culture and in this respect are quite different from their English counterparts. The English novelist has worked from within, cherishing the very institution he or she mocks while the American writer, whether in romantic or realistic fiction diverges, moving along outside institutions and history.

It is also an error to speak of the post war period as if it possessed a unified character. Each decade witnesses shifts in the personal tone of the novelists as public policy and socio-cultural setup changes. Thus the late-forties, the years immediately following the war were the years when the world was trying to recover from the aftermath of the war, the Marshall plan tried to put a balm on the shattered economy of Europe and the Doomsday bomb left a deep scar on the psyche of human beings. Norman Mailer's *The Naked and the Dead*, Irwin Shaw's *The Young Lions* and James Jones's *From Here To Eternity* depicted the horrors of war, the evils of Fascism and the totalitarianism of the army.

The 1950s opened with the suspicious Cold War as the anti-Communist and Leftist hysteria whipped up passions in America even as writers like Norman Mailer continued to show sympathy towards Leftist ideologies. In the 1950s a new social order began to emerge in America with debates about the concepts of culture and individualism. Historian Godfrey Hodgson contends that the decade was marked by a political and social consensus that he has dubbed as the 'liberal ideology' that consisted of a commitment to anti-Communism and free enterprise (Hodgson, 491). Furthermore, historian Loren Baritz is of the opinion that the 50s were a decade of technological revolution. It was also an era of questioning.

If the 1950s was an era of questioning and coming of a new social order, the 1960s were politically very active. Kennedy came to power in 1961 and the country regained youthful consciousness of itself. But this euphoria was short-lived and with Kennedy's assassination in 1963, a new kind of violence and insanity gripped the nation. The Civil Rights Movement and assassination of Martin Luther King tore the country asunder and America was dragged further into the quagmire of the Vietnam War. There was widespread disillusionment as individuals from all walks of life began to lose faith and trust in America's institutions. Once again the novelist responded to these social changes. Joseph Heller's *Catch 22* was published in 1962. The novel was not only an attack on World War II but also an assault on the Vietnam War and other wars fought by America.

The 1970s were also politically active, although not as active as the 1960s. This was the era of Nixon Administration and a breakthrough in the Cold War occurred when Nixon travelled to Peking and Moscow. However, many people became confused and disheartened by the clash between a Vietnam and Cold War rhetoric that painted Communism as the destroyer of individual liberties and governmental actions which seemed expressly designed to squelch individual freedom on the home front. The turbulent crosscurrents of this contradictory state of affairs have been examined by many of the war novels, especially Heller's *Catch 22* which censures the American government for its false piety, hypocrisy and false commitment towards democratic values. Once again the invasion of Cambodia was strongly protested against by novelists who were strongly critical of American attempts at maintaining hegemony over the weaker nations. Vonnegut's *Slaughterhouse Five* was published in 1969.

The war novel therefore developed as a novel of protest due to the above social factors. The novelist stubbornly refused to promote America as a superhero who had won the war and emerged out of it as the most powerful nation. Nor did they glorify the war and the role played by America in annihilating the Fascists from the world. Apart from these social factors there were other important influences that helped in the development of the war novel as a genre.

One of the important influences on the war novel was the theory of Existentialism, which came to America from France in the 1950s. Existentialism is a philosophical movement that views human existence as having a set of underlying themes and characteristics, such as anxiety, dread, freedom, awareness of death, and consciousness of existing. These are primary themes and cannot be reduced to or explained by a natural-scientific approach or any approach that attempts to detach itself from or rise above these themes. Human beings are exposed to or, to use the philosopher Martin Heidegger's phrase, 'thrown' into existence in a world that is meaningless and absurd. Existentialists consider being thrown into existence as prior to, and the horizon or context of, any other thoughts or ideas that humans have or definitions of themselves that they create. Sartre, one of the founders of Existentialism also upholds this idea. The theory conceives of Being itself as something that can only be understood through and in relation to these basic characteristics of human existence. For Existentialists human beings can be understood only from the inside, in terms of their lived and experienced reality and dilemmas and not from the outside, in terms of a biological, psychological, or other scientific theory of human nature. It emphasizes action, freedom, and decision as fundamental to human existence. Existentialism rejects all of the Western rationalist definitions of Being in terms of a rational principle. It tends to view human beings as subjects in an indifferent, often ambiguous, and 'absurd' universe in which meaning is not provided by either the natural order or God but rather can be created, however provisionally and unstably, by human beings' actions and interpretations. The Existentialists also focus upon Man seeking a sense of self in an absurd world.

War literature of the 1950s and 60s focuses on the Existential dilemma of Man. The individual caught in conflict is an isolated subject faced with the absurdity of action in a meaningless world. Paul Christie is of the opinion that:

> "At best, a character in these novels manages moments of self-awareness or Existential heroism-accepting existence and the responsibility of his own freedom

> while finding the power of will within himself that enables him to act without relying upon society. Characteristically, the results are Sisyphean. A good example of this is found in John Dos Passos's *Three Soldiers*. In this novel, Dos Passos sees the self as isolated and alienated by automaton conformity. His protagonist John Andrews, makes a bid to stand free and alone, but ultimately, his solitary action proves futile. World War II novelist Joseph Heller shows us another quixotic gesture in *Catch 22*, in which Yossarian finally takes a stand for personal, Existential freedom against impossible odds. Likewise, Norman Mailer's Lieutenant Hearn in *The Naked and the Dead* and James Jones's Private Prewitt in *From Here to Eternity* attempt to be free and responsible individuals by quixotically tilting with the windmills of the military monolith." (Christie, 70)

Howard M. Harper believes that the crisis in the culture of the fifties was an Existential crisis. The theme of self-discovery that runs through the fiction of this period reveals the intense preoccupation of the writers with the problem of self. It reveals the struggle to define and shape a relationship between self and the American culture (Harper, 108). The predicament of war drives the protagonist deep into his own resources, forcing him to face himself and to examine his principles with unprecedented scrutiny. The intensity of the experience detailed in the war novels crystallizes individual values and produces self-evaluation, an important theme in many of these novels. During and since World War II, the anxious, alienated, individuals have been a focus of attention. Existentialist philosophers, most notably, Jean-Paul Sartre, have frequently discussed isolated individuals.

In consonance with the theory of Existentialism novelists used the technique of Black Humour to convey their horror of war. Black Humour is a device used in literature, drama, and film and is grotesque or morbid humour used to express the absurdity, insensitivity, paradox, and cruelty of the modern world. Ordinary characters or situations are usually exaggerated far beyond the limits of normal satire or irony. Max Schulz is of the opinion that: "Black Humour is a phenomenon of the 1960s, comprising a group of writers who share a viewpoint and an aesthetics for pacing off the boundaries of a nuclear-powered, war-saturated, chemically oriented world" (Schulz, 30). Black Humour uses devices often associated with tragedy and is sometimes equated with tragic farce. For example, Stanley Kubrick's film *Dr. Strangelove Or: How I Learned to Stop Worrying and Love the Bomb* is a terrifying comic treatment of the circumstances surrounding the dropping of an atom bomb, while Jules Feiffer's comedy *Little Murders* is a delineation of the horrors of modern urban life, focusing particularly on random assassinations.

Writers like Heller and Vonnegut used Black Humour, humour with a sinister undercurrent to convey these ideas in their novels. Yossarian, the hero of Heller's *Catch 22* and Billy Pilgrim the hero of Vonnegut's *Slaughterhouse Five* are constantly engaged in comical attempts for survival in 'a crazy world'. Heller's novel is a piece of black comedy and deals with the attempts of Air Force captain Yossarian to stay alive and sane through bombing missions, that never seem to come to an end. Serious and satirical, the novel creates a surreal universe of drollery and death. Vonnegut's most famous novel *Slaughterhouse Five* also makes use of similar techniques. The novel centers on the Allied firebombing of Dresden during World War II and Vonnegut presents this drama of death using Black Humour. Laughter and tears are juxtaposed in both these novels. Schulz believes that Black Humour is painful laughter with "a wink so tight that it brings an emphatic tear to the eyes of both the author and the reader" (Schulz, 32).

In the late 1960s traditional techniques of fiction especially realistic fiction suddenly seemed obsolete and irrelevant with writers like John Barth talking about the Literature of Exhaustion. The complexities of the modern age were impossible to capture in a conventionally realist style and more experimental ways of writing were needed in order to portray the chaos and disorder of the world after the Second War. Therefore postmodernist authors like Thomas Pynchon, Raymond Federmen, Donald

Bartheleme, Kurt Vonnegut and Joseph Heller turned away from realistic fiction to experiment with new styles of writing.

The novels of postmodernist writers like Vonnegut can be termed as an example of metafiction. Metafiction can be described as fiction about the nature and purpose of fiction, which attempts to blur the line between fiction and reality. According to Patricia Waugh a work of this sort lays bare the conventions of fiction and draws attention to language and literary styles that it uses. Under this type of writing, novelists often break out of the narrative to address the nature of what they are doing in the novel. Victoria Orlowski is of the opinion that the writers of metafiction employ what is called the metafictive devices in their writing. For instance, novelists directly addressing the reader, interrupt the narrative to comment on the writing, openly questioning how narrative assumptions and conventions transform and filter reality. These novelists also rely on unconventional and experimental techniques such as rejection of conventional plot, and a display of reflexivity.

Although the term metafiction gained currency during the 1980s, its terminological validity is still contested. In the 1970s and 1980s most critics who explored the development of experimental writing in America felt compelled to invent their own terminology and soon terms such as self-reflexive fiction, surfiction, introverted fiction and the like were competing for acceptance among critics. Orlowski believes that:

> "Initially, it was, however, the postmodern foregrounding of the constructedness of all forms of 'world making' as well as its rejection of the dominant master-narratives that seemed to relate metafiction directly to the avant-garde of the 1960s and 70s. In the wake of the postmodernist questioning of traditional concepts of identity, reality, meaning and representation this avant-garde began to voice a fundamental distrust of the old verities, and affirmed the provisionality and indeterminacy of the modes of comprehending the world." (Orlowski, 1)

In self-consciously displaying the fictional nature of all representations of reality, metafictionists pointed out that our knowledge of the world is always comprehended through language and the cultural predispositions by which language determines our re-constructions of reality. Yet, if the relationship between language and the phenomenal world is already highly problematic, then our seemingly mimetic representations of reality in the arts are even more so. By explicitly commenting on the processes of fiction making, metafiction not only displays the arbitrariness of the linguistic system, but also insists on the impossibility of gaining access to 'objective' reality.

Ronald Sukenick's writing about the post-realistic novel in *The Death of the Novel and Other Stories* directly relates the rise of new fictional forms to the post-realistic, i.e. postmodern, frame of mind. Sukenick and his fellow metafictionists turned man's inability to grasp and represent reality to their own advantage and regarded the collapse of traditional notions of reality as a means of liberation, of allowing the human imagination to transcend the limitations formerly imposed by narrow categories of coherence and plausibility. Writers of postmodern metafiction thus often comment on their failure to construct a coherent fictional reality while, at the same time, rejoicing in the creative freedom this failure generates. The postmodern fiction writer whose old notions of reality have proven inadequate and who, according to Sukenick, is thus forced to start from scratch, is no longer trapped in the situation of a total exhaustion of literary conventions, but finds himself called upon to create a new what John Barth calls 'literature of replenishment'.

While war novelists like Vonnegut and Heller adopted avant-garde styles of writing, Mailer and Jones writers of the late 1940s and 50s continued to be influenced by the old literary tradition of Naturalism. The term Naturalism describes a type of literature that attempts to apply scientific principles of objectivity and detachment to its study of human beings. The founder of this philosophy Emile Zola believed that human beings are, 'human beasts', characters that can be studied through relationships to their surroundings. Zola's description of this method in *Le Roman Experimental (The Experimental Novel)* follows Claude Bernard's medical model and the historian Hippolyte Taine's observation that virtue and vice are products like vitriol and sugar and human beings, as 'products' should be studied impartially, without moralizing about their natures.

Through this objective study of human beings, Naturalistic writers believed that the laws behind the forces that govern human lives could be studied and understood. These writers thus used scientific method to write their novels and believed that forces of heredity and environment determined the lives of human beings. In George Becker's famous and much-annotated and contested phrase, Naturalism's philosophical framework can be simply described as 'pessimistic materialistic determinism' (Becker, 2). Another critic Eric Sundquist comments, that reveling in the extraordinary, the excessive, and the grotesque in order to reveal the immutable bestiality of Man in Nature, Naturalism dramatizes the loss of individuality at a physiological level by making a Calvinism without God its determining order and violent death its Utopia (Sudquist, 5). According to Donald Pizer:

> "The Naturalist often describes his characters as though they are conditioned and controlled by environment, heredity, instinct, or chance. But he also suggests a compensating humanistic value in his characters or their fates, which affirms the significance of the individual and his life. The tension here is that between the Naturalist's desire to represent in fiction the new, discomfiting truths which he has found in the ideas and life of his late nineteenth-century world, and also his desire to find some meaning in experience which reasserts the validity of the human enterprise." (Pizer, 2)

In addition to these strands present in the Naturalistic novel, it is also important to note that most of these writers were critics of capitalism and materialism. Writers like Frank Norris, Upton Sinclair, Theodore Dreiser, John Steinbeck, Dos Passos and others were critical of American avarice. The picture of life that emerges from Naturalist fiction is sordid and depressing. Characters drift about aimlessly, fail, or simply remain trapped in an oppressive environment. They are often ill educated or belong to the lower classes and their attempts at exercising free will or choice are hamstrung by forces beyond their control. There is a special disillusionment with America and behind the relentless examination of contemporary society is the fear that America did not provide the liberty, equality and chance of happiness that it had promised.

It is important to study the history behind the growth of the Naturalist novel in America in order to understand how this movement became an integral part of war literature. The movement is inextricably linked to the growth of capitalism. The latter half of the nineteenth century saw the development of urbanization in America with an increasing number of its citizens becoming city-dwellers. The formerly rural and agrarian American nation rapidly became an urban and industrial country. The proliferation of intercontinental railroad lines and telegraphs helped open new national markets for industry and agriculture and small-scale farmers began to be squeezed out by increasingly mechanized agricultural processes, and many rural folk started to feel that impersonal forces, such as bankers, commodities traders, and railroad barons, were controlling them, as small farms and the small towns they supported declined, displaced or ambitious rural people looking for a better life flocked to the cities to fill the many industrial jobs created by the new markets. It was during this period that Naturalist writers like Frank Norris and Jack London began to make their presence felt on the American literary scene. This shift in the nation's cultural and economic focus was coincident with a shift in the intellectual atmosphere emanating from Europe.

Paul Christie believes that the chief agent of this intellectual ferment was the publication by Charles Darwin of *The Origin of the Species* and *The Descent of Man*. The evolutionary theory advanced by Darwin shook the traditional religious faith of many as uncertainty and skepticism gained sway. Herbert Spencer then applied Darwin's notion of the survival of the fittest to the social realm, and others began seeing Capitalism, in the light of Darwinism, as another manifestation of survival of the fittest. As the influence of biological and social Darwinism on American thought spread, a deterministic view of the world began to gain adherence amongst the general public.

Writing at the same time as Darwin and Spencer was Karl Marx. Although his works *The Communist Manifesto* and *Das*

Kapital did not receive the immediate attention that Darwin's work did, Marx's economic determinism was certainly influential by the turn of the century. In contrast to Marx's meliorist vision, Sigmund Freud presented a more pessimistic strain of determinism in the early part of the twentieth century. He saw the individual as a being ruled by psychic forces generally beyond her or his control.

All these deterministic ideas contributed to the rise of Naturalism, which helped spread these concepts well beyond the intellectual community. Christie is of the opinion that in this Naturalistic version of the individual, the autonomous self is illusory and people are nothing but the expression of their hungers, fears, and environment. Free choice is not possible and choice depends upon economic necessities, psychic drives, or the indoctrination of our social upbringing. These deterministic ideas after being applied to a criticism of Capitalism began to be exemplified on the battlefields of the First World War, impressing upon soldiers their own human powerlessness and, ultimately, helping to define the ethos of the century to come.

Prior to World War I, considerable dissatisfaction with an increasingly materialistic America already existed. According to Stanley Cooperman, disenchanted young men were eager to embrace the war as a way to realize their ideals and add adventure, purpose, and meaning to their lives. They hoped to emulate Stephen Crane's Henry Fleming and achieve manhood on the battlefield. Unfortunately, what the war gave them in return for their enthusiasm was mud, trenches, and indiscriminate carnage, which only served to deepen their disenchantment, rather than dissipating it as they had hoped.

After the war the literary modernists broached the vision of a world gone mad. The Hungarian critic, George Lucas, maintains 'there is a continuity from Naturalism to the Modernism of our day'. Lucas sees in Naturalism a 'dim anticipation of approaching catastrophe' which after 1914 develops into an 'all-pervading obsession' for the modernists (Lucas, 487). The modernist version of the self arose primarily from the waste and slaughter of World War I.

This idea continued in the war novel of the Second Great War. In the view of many writers, the anomie, fragmentation, and isolation of the individual revealed by World War I had endured throughout the century and had been demonstrated anew with each successive war. Consequently, many twentieth-century authors followed the lead of the novelists of World War I using the battlefield as the stage upon which to work out their explorations of what it meant to be an individual in the twentieth century, an individual ensnared in the mass culture of the modern industrial world. Building on the tradition of Naturalism, the fiction of war novelists details the harsh realities of warfare especially the soldier's helplessness and portrays various individuals reacting to its challenges. Christie argues that all novelists envision a meaningless world, but some seem to focus solely on the Naturalistic elements of individual experiences, seeing nothing but solitary, isolated individuals overwhelmed by circumstance. Others allow rare individuals to experience moments of self-awareness but extremely brief, of certainty amid the chaotic flux.

The War novelists portray individuals who are irredeemably at the mercy of circumstances beyond their understanding or control. Unlike the rare self-aware person, most of these individuals believe they are already free and they have no idea of the extent to which their lives are determined by an indifferent universe. Writing about World War II, Norman Mailer and James Jones amplify this deterministic motif. Mailer's *The Naked and the Dead* envisions a meaningless, naturalistic world in which the so-called 'rugged individual' is non-existent. Those who aspire to that state, such as Mailer's Sergeant Croft, are inevitably thwarted by circumstance, as Croft is by a hornet's nest. James Jones works the theme of social constraint and coercion to the full in *The Thin Red Line*. His characters Bell and Welsh see the individual as insignificant and of little interest or worth to anyone but himself, and his characters Doll and Fife are shown to be nothing but a reflection of the opinions of others.

In keeping with the tradition of the Naturalists, *The Naked and the Dead* is also an incisive critique of American society and the American culture of abundance. In fact in the novel the evils of fascism are equated with the evils of Capitalism (when he was writing this novel Mailer had Leftist leanings). After having indicted the capitalistic American society, Mailer suggests that there are certain neurotic disabilities present in Americans, which are induced by the culture itself. In Mailer's opinion United States is a seedbed of psychic insecurity. Since *The Naked and the Dead* is a war novel, Mailer takes the American soldier as a case in point. He criticizes American society by introducing a device called the Time Machine, which enables him to flashback the civilian life of his soldiers. He explains their actions and attitudes in the army is a result of the oppressive environment prevailing in society. Among the psychological problems created by society, the most obvious is racial and religious discrimination. Soldiers like Martinez, the Mexican Sergeant and the Jew Goldstein feel alienated on account of being minority groups.

Discipline is an essential feature of the army but its extreme implementation led to totalitarianism, which was looked upon as the infringement of individual liberty. This authoritarianism has also been criticized in the novels of the Second World War. Historian Denis Brogan is of the opinion that the Americans of the 1930s and 1940s were antimilitary. In his book *Studies in Social Psychology in World War II* Brogan argues that most men who were conscripted into the army during the war looked upon it as a forced disturbance of normal patterns of personal life. Most of them failed to achieve a satisfactory relationship with the military organization or a reasonable understanding of their own role in the nation's war aims neither making any personal commitment to the war nor displaying any enthusiasm towards combat. During training and on the battlefront soldiers resented the rigorous discipline of the army and the tyranny of officers who did not allow individuals to exercise any sort of freedom. The war novelist was sensitive to injustice and compassionate towards those who were wronged by the military machine. This concern for the oppressed, enlisted man called the 'dog soldier' stemmed from the attitudes that the novelists had inherited from the 1930s, which was primarily a decade of social protest in America. The rebellion against mindless arbitrary authority, which had been directed against the police in the 1930s, was directed in the war novels against the officer class. *The Naked and the Dead* is a criticism of the totalitarianism of the army that reduces the individual to a state of oblivion.

War establishes its own universe of relationship and sensations, different from those in civilian life. Men are transformed into mechanical objects, by fear and a desire for survival. Superior officers like General Cummings and the high command have placed a wall around individual need and desire and their minds and sensations are severely constrained. All the characters in the novel have been depersonalized by the regimentation of the army and only the character of a soldier named Croft has individuality, and he is Mailer's provisional triumph. For Mailer, Croft represents the perfect individual he has a powerful personality a massive ego, only partially disguised as devotion to the army; a vast struggle between self and anti-self. He displays a vast struggle between strength and weakness and continuously shows a desire to turn everyone and everything to his own will. Karl is of the opinion that he is "pure Being", as against Nothingness, which he brushes. Croft is the ideal, (however unsettling such an ideal may be to the liberal-humanistic mind) of what the army demands.

James Jones's novel *From Here to Eternity*, in its prewar scenes is the war novel equivalent of *The Grapes of Wrath* with the army base in Hawaii substituting for the dust bowl of the Steinbeck novel. Jones's novel is, of course, more than that and its theme encompasses issues like the atomization of the society into class and also deals with themes like political infighting, controlled capitalistic systems and politics of bureaucracy. Although there is no war in most of the novel, it points toward the attack on Pearl Harbour, and when the attack comes, Jones has suggested for us a military society that reflects the larger society. *From Here to Eternity*, uses the peacetime army as a metaphor for society because the army is made up of officers like Dynamite Holmes who were not only despotic but also were members of the bourgeoisie middle class, which had always exploited the poor classes of America.

In the novel Jones reveals how the totalitarian army tries to destroy the individuality of Robert Lee Prewitt an idealist and a 'good' soldier. Howard M. Harper argues that the author attempts a large-scale presentation by ensnaring Prewitt between 'Art' (the bugle), which he gives up, and 'War' (boxing) which he withdraws from formally while remaining a fighter. Frederick Karl is of the opinion that:

> "The conception here is ambiguous, although one can see it, through Jones's eyes as an effort to thrust Prewitt into the larger world, which his lowly role in the army negates. He is, in this larger sense, a young man moving between Art and War, Apollo and Mars, a man who defies the army after he has had his moments of greatness, as bugler and as boxer, and now he comes to us as a legend. Jones's aim was to make him larger than life and he therefore had to provide Prewitt an immortal past, from Kentucky coalfields to the worlds of Art and War." (Karl, 100)

Prewitt's forsaking of Art and War in order to carry on his own kind of war has diminished him as an individual. His past may be glorious, but his present is small scaled and Jones makes an attempt to depict Prewitt's struggle to retain his independence when he has volunteered to work for an organization that punishes individuality. Prewitt is in the army by free choice because it is somehow preferable to coal mining or other demeaning work and yet once within that organization, he insists on antithetical forms of behaviour. The terms of the army are clear-forgo individuality submit to discipline dictated by the organization and show mechanical obedience to superiors. Prewitt however insists upon pursuing his 'free choice'.

Jones shows great sympathy towards the lower-class soldiers in this novel and his other novels like *The Thin Red Line*, and *Whistle*. Through his novels he expresses the opinion that whatever good feeling of honesty derives from army life, derives from the lower-class soldier, the lower soldier moves along the margins of the army and makes great sacrifices during combat situations.

Karl is of the opinion that there is a great amount of romanticism in this belief, such as one finds in Dos Passos's biographical insets in U.S.A. Jones is of the opinion that the 'dog soldier' makes valuable contribution to the army. However, he is highly contemptuous of the officer class, the 'other' class that is made up officers like Dynamite Holmes.

Jones's *The Thin Red Line* depicts brutal hand to hand combat in the forests of Guadalcanal and he uses enclosed space and time, restricted cast of characters, equally limited area of maneuver, no meaningful ideology, stark tensions and conflicts, mainly fear to make his work extremely powerful. In *The Thin Red Line* Jones writes about a real campaign, the Guadalcanal campaign and the governing idea of this intense, brutal novel is that an army is the gigantic maw or stomach, something that will consume all who enter and replace them with identical pieces, until they in turn are consumed. Large parts of Jones's novel are concerned with the relocating of men as they assume different titles within the company and take the place of men who are killed in combat. Men are used as links, as objects with a total disregard for their feelings. The army in wartime combat is the perfect vehicle for what the author only suggested in *From Here to Eternity*. It presents the point of view of the marginal or 'dog' soldier; the man whom the army subdues and then usually kills.

The combat on the Island is the most important theme of the novel and it is intensely and brutally narrated, and becomes everything, the entire narrative, plot, theme, characterization, as well as tone, texture, point of view—all the elements we associate with fiction. Many soldiers die during combat but are quickly replaced by more men and this cycle recurs until the army's gigantic stomach has consumed all the participants. Meanwhile, a new batch is preparing to step in. "Those who did not die would be entered upon the elaborate shuttling movement back out from this furthermost point of advance, as only a short time back they had been entered upon the shuttle forward into it" (*TRL*, 500).

Joseph Heller's *Catch 22* is a novel about the deadly logistics of war, rather than the terrifying tribulations of combat. The novel is a strong critique of the military bureaucracy and the chaotic modern society where wars are endless. *Catch 22* is a black comedy about death and about what people do when faced with the daily likelihood of annihilation in a war torn world. The novel is about an air force squadron in which the men are directly answerable to Colonel Cathcart whose sole preoccupation after survival and sycophancy is getting his photograph into the *Saturday Evening Post.* His strategy is to raise the number of missions his men must fly before being released from combat; from forty-five to seventy to eighty in the course of the novel and he would gladly go on raising the number of missions even up to six thousand if that's what it takes to impress his superiors.

The novel deals with the military bureaucracy and the system, which can stifle an individual. The title of the novel, which entered the English language after the novel was published, refers to a situation where the individual can never emerge as the winner. Catch 22 is a monstrous law that governs the army, (making war possible) and even has its tenacious grip on the modern society as well. It is a law, which destroys the individual through its fallacious reasoning.

Vonnegut's *Slaughterhouse Five* is primarily a novel about war and the cruelty and violence perpetuated during war. One of the important themes of the novel is the moral degeneration of Man and the erosion of basic values like kindness and sympathy, which Vonnegut believes, makes human beings wage wars in the world. Skepticism towards science and technology is also an important issue in the novel as the author puts forth the view that in the contemporary world technology has become a bane for modern man. Science and technology, which was to be used for the benefit of Mankind, is being used for the destruction of humanity and it was technology that led to the annihilation of cities like Dresden, Hiroshima and Nagasaki. Vonnegut's novel examines the devastating impact of war on the civilian population of a country. The author is a pacifist and his pacifist views are the major theme of *Slaughterhouse Five.*

Irwin Shaw's *The Young Lions* is an example of historical fiction. The novel is set against the backdrop of many important historical episodes including battles like the Battle of El Alamein, the London Blitzkrieg, the Occupation and Liberation of Paris and Hitler's forcible union of Austria and Germany called Anschluss. The novel is a strong critique of the Nazi philosophy and its central thematic concern revolves around the battle between good and evil. Irwin Shaw has thus looked upon war as a moral allegory. Christian Diestel, one of the three protagonists of the novel is a Nazi and a cruel monster whose only aim is to kill and destroy the lives of human beings, while Noah Ackerman and Michael Whitacre are the 'good' characters of the novel who want goodness and decency to be restored in the modern war torn world. There are only two combat scenes in the novel. One is set in the deserts of Africa where Shaw describes the war between the German soldiers and the British soldiers and is based on the historical episode of Rommel's (Hitler's General) retreat from Africa. The other combat scene occurs during the famous Normandy Landings when Noah Ackerman the American soldier makes a sensational escape from behind the enemy lines.

The present work deals with only five novelists but there are a myriad variety of books that have been written about the Second World War. An outstanding example of a war novel is John Hawke's *The Cannibal* which presents the grim despair and desperation of war in an interesting manner. The novel is interesting because it moves beyond realism as Hawkes has chosen to express his feelings for the dislocation of the war torn world in a surrealistic manner. Surrealism deserts the ordered, rational world of experience because reason has failed both as an instrument of order and comprehension and plunges below the empirical world of reality with the conviction that reality lies in the subconscious. In the novel, a non-sequential logic dominates the presentation of events, fears and fantasies of childhood colour the gruesome action and an atmosphere of horror pervades the entire environment. Hawkes succeeds in conveying a sense of misery, sterility, destruction, futility and madness. *Williwaw* by Gore Vidal, presents another variety of despair, one found in the purposelessness in the lives of soldiers who do not fight, but wait endlessly for combat. The tension, takes a toll on the nerves of these soldiers. This novel attempts, in the Hemingway manner to record accurately and simply the observed scene, as if only physical detail were of real importance because only that can be trusted.

The fatigue, anxiety and fear of combat are also revealed in a novel called *The Gallery* by John Horne Burns. The novel, which is about a fierce war in Europe and North Africa, has only one combat scene, the war being in fact reflected in men trying to relieve themselves from the exhaustion, nervousness, and dread of combat. There is almost no war except that which can be mirrored in their destructive means of relaxation like drinking, visiting gay and straight bars, and forms of madness which allow withdrawal. The means for Burn's formulation is the vast Galleria Umberto primo in Naples, a temple of glass, which is a fitting symbol of the reflected pleasure that soldiers seek. In Mailer, the long sections on the patrol working behind Japanese lines preempt the shape of the novel, giving it a snakelike, episodic quality with its own tensions and dialectic. In Burns the dominant symbolic shape of the crystal gallery, whose glass has been shattered by Allied bombers, gives him a literal container for the novel, a pleasure dome, a sacred place where black masses occur yet also a church that offers salvation and life but is like the war itself, a magnet for destruction, doom and death.

The war and the combat novels examine the predicament of the beleaguered individual caught in a massive technological confrontation. How the individual retains a sense of self is an important theme in war fiction.

James Jones: The War Trilogy—*From Here to Eternity, The Thin Red Line* and *Whistle*

2

American authors approached the Second World War from many different angles. John Oliver Killen in *And Then We Heard the Thunder* focuses on the struggle of African American soldiers during World War II and the novel is a plea for black unity in the face of segregation, prejudice, and hate. *The War Lover* by John Hersey is a Freudian psychological novel, which tries to comprehend the psyche of Buzz Marrow, a man who loves war. Set in the occupied Italy of 1944, John Horne Burns's *The Gallery* contrasts Old World culture and values with the corrupt values of materialistic American culture, while John Hawkes' *The Cannibal* a surreal novel criticizes war by conveying a sense of misery, sterility, futility and madness.

The mechanized, powerfully destructive nature of warfare had been delineated in the novels of John Dos Passos, Ernest Hemingway and E.E. Cummings, who had written about the First War and had unequivocally portrayed that valour and patriotism were false and non-existent on a battlefield. Many novelists who had participated in the Second World War used the battlefield experience as a means of exploring issues such as the army's absolutism and its impact on the individual soldier. The post war world witnessed what Peter Aichinger calls a great 'ordering' of society. The army was tremendously ordered and disciplined, but such order spilled over into civilian life as well as the Cold War began and the threat of Communism moved the country towards rightist ideologies. Military budgets remained high, and the political influence of the army threatened to erode democracy, and its principles. Therefore, the American ideal of individuality came under threat as people began to feel anxious, insecure, anonymous and insignificant. The works of writers such as Mailer and Jones were reactions, to this threat, as their writing depicts atomized and isolated individuals who are devastated not only by war but also by the oppressive army that crushes their individuality.

James Jones began his career with *From Here to Eternity*, a spectacularly successful novel about World War II. Thereafter he wrote a trilogy comprising two other novels, *The Thin Red Line* and *Whistle* based on his personal experiences in the Second World War. He has often been called a Naturalist and a 'tough' writer who is unable to portray female characters sympathetically in his novels. However, one theme that is persistent in his war trilogy is the animal nature of man and all Jones's characters are doomed by the same interrelated causes; the animal nature of man and the anonymous nature of modern technological society. In an interview the writer stated that all human beings are sadistic and have an animal portion in their temperament, which is not averse to inflicting cruelty on others. He frankly admitted that he too possessed traces of such bestiality.

Jones views modern man as being caught in an external and an internal trap. Human strength, which arises out of our 'animal' nature, has been translated into an awesome technology, which threatens the extinction of all individuality. In such a technological war each soldier becomes an expendable cipher, for while in the army and during actual combat the infantryman has to function as a 'part' of the 'whole' in order to have any chance for survival. Jones depicts an 'all male' world in his novels. But his novels shatter the notion of 'masculinity' as in all the three novels the rugged individual is non-existent and the battlefield is no longer an arena where Man can establish his 'Manhood'. The hero has been replaced by the 'honest coward' who believes that dying for one's country is a foolish enterprise. Further, Jones seems to opine that 'masculinity' leads to animalism which in turn leads to primitivism, cannibalism, fragmentation and loss of identity.

Seeking escape from such anonymity, his characters attempt a retreat to 'frontiers' of individualism only to find the 'frontiers' already threatened by technology and to discover that they cannot escape their own animal heritage. In the course of discovering a last frontier of individual freedom, man, the animal, inevitably perverts and destroys it. Jones is also of the view that war and combat are socially sanctioned outlets for man's animalism. Although throughout his fiction, he endeavours to present apparent escape routes, all of these are dead ends. Thus the author may appear as an extremely cynical individual but he is actually a realist and says that he was always aware that escape could not be attained. The ultimate escape from these limitations was the brutality of combat where man's 'animalism' becomes his main ally. This worldview projected by the author is an extremely depressing one. However, critics like Edmund Volpe are of the view that despite having an embittered and cynical view towards life Jones believes in 'man's enduring and prevailing spirit' (Volpe, 106).

The Second World War can be identified as the source of Jones's bitter vision. Out of the horror of Pearl Harbour and Guadalcanal emerged the theme of the 'Evolution of the soldier' that clearly rests upon the novelist's concept of man's 'animal nature'. The army systematically dehumanizes the enlisted man to prepare him for the necessary anonymity of combat. The final anonymity potentially faced by every soldier in wartime is death. World War II represented the peak of man's utilization of technology for the purpose of destruction and in such a technological war, each soldier became even more of an expendable, anonymous cipher. The army using its awareness of man's inherent animalism carried out its dehumanization process and the war trilogy illustrates the effects of such a process on the enlisted man. Thus every experience of the draftee was designed to destroy his sense of self. A combat soldier had not only to know but also to accept the fact that as an individual, he had ceased to exist at the time of his induction. The actual battle experience completed the process of dehumanization as combat brought home the final anonymity of death. James Giles is of the opinion that a central moment in an infantrymen's evolution came when he had no chance to survive. Some men would survive, of course, but the odds made it clear that the individual would not. In actual combat, the infantryman had to function as a selfless 'part' of the 'whole' to have any chance for temporary survival. He constantly saw the men around him die brutally at the hands of the enemy and chance. Any lingering vestiges of a civilized morality were sacrificed when he killed in an equally brutal manner.

The acceptance of the reduction of the self to 'an animalistic cipher' is a trauma for characters like Prewitt, Witt and Landers in Jones's war trilogy. After the war, the United States had produced a new kind of man, one who accepted the inevitability of his own death and the suspension of western morality in which he had been raised. If he survived the war, he had to return home and begin the process of De-evolution of a soldier. This too was a difficult experience. Thus Jones reveals the evolution of the soldier in *From Here to Eternity* (pre-war peace time army), the experience of a soldier in *The Thin Red Line* (Guadalcanal combat) and the disintegration of a soldier in *Whistle* (the embittered returning soldier). This view of the soldier is derived from Jones's own participation in the war and his own experience as a soldier. In the introductory 'note' to *Whistle* Jones informs his readers that he wished the three novels to be seen as a special kind of trilogy:

> "It was always my intention with this trilogy that each novel should standby itself as a work alone. In a way that, for example, John Dos Passos's three novels in his fine USA trilogy do not. *The 42nd Parallel*, *1919* and *The Big Money* will not stand alone as novels. *USA* is one large novel, not a trilogy." (*Whistle*, i)

Partly to insure this intention, Jones decided to carry three character types through all three novels, but to give them different names in each volume in order to symbolize the changes circumstance and environment had produced in them. Thus, the rebellious Private is Prewitt in *From Here to Eternity*, Witt in *The Thin Red Line* and Prell in *Whistle*, the strong competent First Sergeant is Warden in the first novel, Welsh in the second and Winch in the third. *From Here to Eternity's* Mess Sergeant Stark first merges into Storm in *The Thin Red Line*, then Strange in *Whistle*. The device is effective because the three become different men under different conditions, while consistently representing a basic character type i.e. the dehumanized soldier. Critics are of the opinion that as a trilogy, the novels constitute the most sustained and thorough examination of the twentieth century soldier and of World War II.

From Here to Eternity: The Evolution of a Soldier

In his journal on the Vietnam War Jones wrote that he viewed *From Here to Eternity* as the first volume in a trilogy on World War II and the experience of a soldier. The novel is thus an introduction to the theme of the evolution of a soldier and is dedicated to the United States Army. Much of the emotional impact of this novel derives from Jones's application of his concept of unavoidable anonymity to Rober E. Lee Prewitt and Milton Anthony Warden. *From Here to Eternity* is not a combat novel and the war i.e. the attack on Pearl Harbour only happens towards the end but Jones depicts the growing parallel between modern technological warfare and the quality of contemporary life. Civilization grows increasingly dependent on technology both in war as well as peace. Waging war, nations exploit the ultimate possibilities of science to further military and political goals. Peter G. Jones is of the view that: "In the twentieth century, therefore, with the boundaries between 'war' and 'peace' nebulous and ill-defined, the war novel is a logical medium for writing about life" (Jones, 73). The novel, which won the National Book Award in 1951, records army life in Schofield Barracks in Hawaii. This organization shown in the novel harbours and encourages totalitarianism and absolutism functioning on the basis of a rigid officer-enlisted men cadre system where the enlisted men are victimized by the officers. It is interesting to note that the army is looked upon as a metaphor for the capitalistic American society in the novel. Just as the bourgeoisie oppress the poor classes in the American social setup, the army too is composed of middle class officers who continuously exploit the 'dog' soldier. Hence Jones's novel is also a critique of capitalism as a system that dehumanizes individuals and the author displays proletarian sympathies and Leftist leanings. The two main protagonists of the story are

Robert E. Lee Prewitt, and Sergeant Milt Warden, men who are destroyed by the inflexibility of the organization. Both these men are good soldiers, never shirking their duties but despotism proves to be their Nemesis.

The novel is divided into five sections: Book one titled *The Transfer* deals with the protagonist Prewitt's reassignment from the Bugle Corps to 'G Company'; a man of significant talents and an idealist, Prewitt doggedly refuses to succumb to the army system. He joined the army in order to escape excruciating poverty and in this organization he is assigned to the Bugle Corps but has himself transferred to 'G Company' headed by the corrupt officer Dynamite Holmes. This happens when he is dislodged as the number one bugler and views this action as unfair and wrong, deliberately seeking a transfer because the idealist that he is, he would never submit to injustice. Initially he tries to explain to the officers who are responsible for his displacement that their action is unfair but when this fails he insists upon a transfer, which begins his war with the brutal system. The opening section of the novel introduces us to other characters like Sergeant Milt Warden, Dynamite Holmes, Maylon Stark, the Mess Sergeant and Karen Holmes, Dynamite's victimized wife.

Book Two of the novel titled *The Company* describes in detail Dynamite Holmes as a corrupt, power hungry officer who does not regard the soldiers in his Company as human beings but looks upon them as 'numbers' or replaceable parts of the army. Since the army shown in the novel is not engaged in conflict, the self-preening officers are occupied in inane and violent activities like boxing. Prewitt is asked to participate in a boxing match being organized by Dynamite Holmes's Company, because the latter is obsessed with winning a boxing trophy which would place him in a coveted position as compared to his colleagues, but the soldier refuses as he once blinded a man while boxing and vowed to his dying mother that he will never hurt anyone intentionally. This enrages the egotistical Holmes, who decides to give the obdurate soldier 'The Treatment'. Prewitt is thrown into the army prison or Stockade and is endlessly and mercilessly tortured. Critics have described this section of the novel titled 'The Stockade' as its most brutal segment. There are disturbing scenes devoted to the army prison in this section as the author shows the 'Stockade' to be a chamber of horrors where prisoners are subjected to the worst kind of persecution. Unable to tolerate the treatment meted out to himself and his fellow prisoners, Prewitt murders the prison guard Fatso Judson and runs away joining Alma the prostitute whom he intends to marry. However, Pearl Harbour is attacked and the 'good soldier' consumed by a patriotic desire to fight for his country decides to return to the organization that has caused him tremendous torment. But while returning to the barracks he is killed by an army guard. Ironically, the guard mistakes Prewitt for an 'intruder'.

The other soldier who is a focus of attention in the novel is Sergeant Milton Warden, who is asked to give Prewitt 'The Treatment' because of his refusal to enter the boxing competition. Basically a fair man, Warden, is torn between his duty to the system and his growing personal feeling for Prewitt, which is ultimately, transformed into friendship as the two men share several attributes like honesty and devotion towards the organization, which is involved in their destruction. Initially, he does participate in torturing Prewitt, but gradually as he comes to admire the soldier, he fights to protect him and when Prewitt dies Warden makes sure that his record reads 'killed in the line of duty'. Warden's hatred of the officer class compels him to seduce Karen Holmes, Dynamite Holmes's wife who has the reputation of being easy. Since Holmes is a symbol of corruption in the army Warden who looks upon Karen, as an extension of her husband and fights corruption by seducing her. However, Karen soon forces him to recognize that she is a victim of, rather than a participant in Dynamite Holmes's corruption. In a hotel room, when Warden cruelly assaults her with the accusation spread by the Company's Mess Sergeant Maylon Stark that she is notoriously promiscuous Karen first speaks of her hatred for men and then tells Warden that she had to undergo a hysterectomy because of an infection from her husband's venereal disease. She explains to him that after the hysterectomy: "you're still not a woman any more...you're not anything. You're a gutted shell" (*Eternity,* 332).

Warden falls in love with Karen, but is unable to take the relationship to its logical culmination as with the coming of the attack on Pearl Harbour he has to kill his individuality and desire, and sink into the anonymity of being a soldier. As is often the case in Jones's novels the characters' names reveal something about their personality. Thus Alma, which means fostering, nurturing, is the refuge for Prewitt that allows him to withstand 'the treatment'. Prewitt named after the Confederate General, is the idealistic hero in a losing cause and Warden is a keeper torn between the system he serves and the men who make it up. Richard P. Adams is of the opinion that the structure of *From Here To Eternity* resembles the letter X, with the two lines of the letter becoming a symbol of two soldiers who represent personal and social approaches to moral integrity. The upward and downward movement of the letter indicates the rise and fall in the fortunes of these two soldiers (Adams, 210).

The novel shows a great concern for the dog soldier especially in the section titled 'Re-enlistment Blues'. This section also emphasizes the idea that artistic creation can never survive in a system where individuality is deliberately killed. *From Here To Eternity* is an army novel but not really a war novel, since World War II begins only as the novel ends. Nevertheless violence is at a high pitch from the beginning till the end. From a character named Bloom's suicide to Fatso Judson's brutal beating of prisoners and Prewitt's murder of Judson to Prewitt's death at the hands of the military police, everything is a brutal test of manhood. In this world, 'maleness' becomes an aggressive need to retain the individual's sanity and though in this aggressively male world women are sexual symbols, Jones portrays the two women characters sympathetically. Karen Holmes's relationship with Warden has already been mentioned. Initially Prewitt embarks upon a relationship with Alma for purely sexual reasons, but later falls in love with her as she provides succour and acts as a poultice on his wounded soul.

The novel is a most realistic and forceful account of life in the army and it's naturalistically rendered scenes of internal army violence, the most brutal in Second World War fiction are conveyed in a tone of genuine outrage. Critics are of the view that the war novels of James Jones differ from Mailer's work because they present an extremely bleak vision of the universe. Whereas Mailer leaves readers with an inkling of hope, Jones leaves us with the depressing feeling that the individual is totally insignificant in the modern world. Therefore, the army becomes a target of attack in *From Here To Eternity*. Captain Dynamite Holmes's G. Company has assumed the identity of a 'single personality', leading to the suppression of individual identities of its other members. Most soldiers of this company have learned to compromise with the situation realizing that their anonymity is the only means of survival in this tyrannical institution. However, the 'thirty-year' soldier and the intensely individualistic rebel Prewitt through his stubborn refusal to compromise takes up a cudgel with the system.

A distinctive characteristic of Prewitt's personality that clashes with the army is his idealism. The soldier is aware that the army is a fraudulent organization but he vows to remain pure within the confines of such an institution at the cost of extreme suffering. His seeking a transfer from the Bugle Corps was also based on his strict code of idealism. Prewitt's refusal to box in order to win the boxing trophy for Dynamite Holmes is also based on his creed of idealism. Interestingly he has acquired his strict code of personal integrity from the mass medium of the movies: "He had only been a green kid but he had learned from all those pictures to believe in fighting for the underdog, against the top dog. He had even made himself a philosophy of life out of it" (*Eternity*, 275). A popular theme in the films of 1930s was the story of the lone individual struggling against powerful social forces or institutions that were aiming to coerce the individual into conformity or break him in the process. This is what happens to Prewitt ultimately, because he has embraced an idealism that is rare and exceedingly difficult to live up to and which leaves him with only two options: resist as an individual or conform as an automaton. The source of Prewitt's idealism is his suffering. While delineating the story of his life Jones describes it as a sordid saga of 'scars': "He had lots of scars...there were scars he had got on the county road gang in Georgia, and the scars he had got from the police" (*Eternity*, 676). As the son of a Harlan County miner, Prewitt had faced excruciating poverty and a difficult childhood but his suffering had not made him cynical and vindictive. While undergoing 'The treatment' at the notorious Stockade a shocked Prewitt realizes that he himself would never have caused another human being so much pain. The army however, has no sympathy for such impractical idealists and makes a brutal assault on Prewitt's dignity and individuality by throwing him into the Stockade.

The Stockade sections of the novel are the most brutal and powerful and extremely frightening. James Giles is of the view that:

> "The Stockade operates in the novel as a symbolic microcosm of the army's corruption. Jones's juxtaposition of hideous brutality with official bureaucratic assaults upon the dignity of the self causes these scenes to be reminiscent of the excesses of Nazi Germany, a parallel intended to be drawn indirectly, but strikingly." (Giles, 183)

The chapters stand out as among the most memorable in the whole of Second World War fiction, and are imaginatively intended as a vindication of Prewitt's rebellious attitude, since they show in its clearest form the oppression of the enlisted man by the discipline of fear. Here the novelist makes his most profound affirmation of human endurance and heroism in his portrayal of the men lodged in Number Two Barracks, the soldiers who make an attempt to defy their punishment and in the process undergo severe hardships. Prewitt's initial experience of the army Stockade is an introduction to Major Thompson, the prison in-charge and the 'grub hoe handle torture'. This officer is the epitome of barbarity as during interrogation prisoners are beaten in the kidneys by guards armed with the omnipresent grub hoe handle while Thompson provides the 'philosophical' justification of the Stockade's brutality thus: "The quickest, efficientest, least expensive way to educate a man is to make it painful for him when he is wrong, the same as with any animal" (*Eternity*, 534). It is shocking that the army looks upon human beings as animals. While undergoing torture, Prewitt notices 'Fatso' Judson, the sadistic and cruel prison guard who takes great pleasure in cruelly beating the prisoners. Prewitt bravely and even heroically endures his trauma at the prison but the violence seems endless as he is whipped and at the orders of the vicious Dynamite Holmes is even incarcerated in a dark cell enduring what is called 'solitary confinement', a punishment reserved for hardened criminals. However, his tolerance reaches a nadir when the morally and ethically depraved Fatso Judson supervises the murder of a man named 'Blues' Berry. The murder of Berry is the worst violation of Prewitt's mother's creed of never hurting anybody and the 'literalist' can see no way of correcting this wrong except by killing him. After Judson's murder, a badly wounded Prewitt deserts the army, and takes refuge in his mistress Alma's arms, vowing never to return. However, Pearl Harbour is attacked and it is one of the novel's sharpest ironies that one of two 'good soldiers', is isolated from the army at this most crucial juncture and in a totally inebriated state sleeps through the actual attack. However Prewitt's idealism and values reassert themselves once he learns of the attack. His farewell scene with Alma is one of the most powerful moments in the novel where Alma makes an attempt to dissuade Prewitt from going back to an institution that has caused him tremendous misery.

> "What do you want to go back to the Army for...what did the army even do for you? Besides beat you up...and throw you in jail like criminal?" "What do I want to go back for?" Prewitt said wonderingly. "I'm a soldier." (*Eternity*, 779-80)

Jones looks upon Prewitt as a symbol of artistic creation. The poet is a bugler par excellence but an organization, which is devoted to annihilation, of individuality cannot appreciate Prewitt's art. Art and creativity is an anathema to totalitarianism and Jones treats artistic creativity in a despairingly painful manner in the novel. Prewitt's bugling rises to a transcendental level and when he plays the bugle the soldiers momentarily forget their sorrows. Prewitt plays the 'Taps' on his bugle and those who listen to his mellifluous notes are transported into a different world. Ben Griffith Jr is of the opinion that Prewitt is like a folk hero circumscribed within the limits of a vocation or profession. Prewitt excels in many things he is a poet, knife fighter, musician, philosopher and a soldier. Griffith believes that Jones creates a myth in the novel and the plot is similar to the Antigone-Creon conflict where Antigone must bury her dead brother even though the law of the state prohibits it, but Creon, who symbolizes the system, cannot brook any disorder to the law (Griffith, 4).

Jones's individualistic-idealistic hero who has always taken pride in making the 'right' decisions is ultimately a lonely human being. Prewitt too recognizes his isolation. Jones uses the 'bee' image while describing Prewitt's situation: "a sense of loss and the aloneness, the utter defenselessness that was each man's lot, sealed up in his bee cell from all the others in the world" (*Eternity*, 89). Prewitt is similar to characters like Doss Passos's John Andrews and Hemingway's Frederic Henry because he is true to himself. Prewitt's story can be called an eloquent paean to a concept of individualism rapidly becoming anachronistic in an increasingly bureaucratic society. According to officers in the army Prewitt is a 'Bolshevik', a rebel who refuses to kow-tow before the totalitarian regime of the army.

The other 'good soldier' who is reduced to a non-entity by the totalitarianism of the army is Sergeant Milt Warden. Warden too has a strong sense of individual integrity but realizes that in order to retain one's individuality, it is necessary to appear to adhere to the system. This soldier is therefore a realist unlike Prewitt and understands the functioning of the army and makes an attempt to manipulate the system in various ways. To begin with he creates a complex role for himself and decides to become the best sergeant in Hawaii. He builds a wall around himself and by not feeling and caring he hopes to protect his own psyche against the assault of the army and its 'stinking' corruption. By endeavouring to become a one-dimensional man, he renounces communication with other people and with himself too to some extent. Throughout Schofield Barracks there is the 'legend of Warden', the ultimate top sergeant—tough, hard, demanding and unfeeling. His uncaring cynicism is a mask to protect himself from the disillusionment of having to work for depraved officers like Dynamite Holmes. However, the danger in such suppression of emotion is madness. Warden's spiritual and psychological descent in Jones's next novel *The Thin Red Line* to 'Mad' Welsh is a predictable end. In *From Here to Eternity* he takes the important first step in accepting the necessary anonymity of war and this brings him in conflict with himself.

There are various ways in which Warden manipulates the system to his own advantage. For instance he often plays little games with himself where he sets the rules and strictly abides by them. This is one way of coping with the army's attack upon his individuality. Another way of fighting this monstrous organization is his penchant for manipulating the officers of the Company so that he is at an advantage. Unlike Prewitt, however, Warden never openly challenges the system, always working within it or around it. He seduces Karen Holmes to assert his individuality and shows his hatred for the officer class. In a soliloquy he justifies his action and declares that his affair with Karen is not borne out of:

> "Vengeance, or even retribution, but as an expression of himself, to regain the individuality that Holmes and all the rest of them, unknowing, had taken from him. And he understood suddenly why a man who has lived his whole life working for a corporation might commit suicide simply to express himself, would foolishly destroy himself because it was the only way to prove his own existence." (*Eternity*, 107)

Much to his surprise, he falls in love with Karen Holmes, and this turns out to be a major test of his personal integrity. However, Karen agrees to divorce her husband and marry Warden, on the condition that he must become an officer because she refuses to move down in the world. Despite the fact that he despises the middle class officers Warden appears for the examination, which the enlisted soldiers are required to clear, passes it, receives a commission but tears it up, thereby refusing to compromise his values and become an officer. Once Pearl Harbour is attacked Warden is unable to continue his relationship with Karen and ends it. Jones seems to suggest that individuals like Warden are incapable of having normal relationships with other human beings. In his relationship with Prewitt too Warden cannot bring himself to become a normal, caring human being. Both Prewitt and Warden are so locked in their own self-imposed roles that neither can make a gesture of simple, direct affection or respect for the other and although Warden tries to save Prewitt from the torture perpetrated on him by the army, he fails.

Thus the novel displays Warden and Prewitt as being in a special kind of combat within the army, which causes Prewitt's death and makes Warden lose his individuality and become 'merely' a soldier. This is the first step in 'becoming' a soldier, a non-entity and a dehumanized character sans emotions and feelings. Even if emotions are there he must like Warden suppress them completely and reveal only his animal nature during actual combat in *The Thin Red Line*, the second novel in Jones's trilogy.

The Thin Red Line: The Experience of a Soldier

The next novel in the trilogy, *The Thin Red Line* sets out to debunk the glory of war. Based on Jones's personal experience the novel is set against the backdrop of the historic Guadalcanal campaign in the Philippines where the Japanese and the American forces had fought a long and protracted battle which had proved to be a decisive one in the Pacific theatre of war. The novel depicts terrible jungle warfare and shows the 'animal nature' of man at its worst. The 'C for Charlie' Company is involved in a mopping up campaign in Guadalcanal and their fighting has no place either in the grand design of the war or in the heroism of the ninety characters in the novel almost all of who have monosyllabic names. The men are constantly engaged in battle and although they are different from each other they are not drawn as individuals. Their military targets, "the things the folks back home" read about, have romantic names such as the 'Dancing Elephant', 'The Sea Slug' and the 'Giant Boiled Shrimp'. In order to demythologize warfare, the novel has no outstanding heroes, but instead the reader's attention is spread through almost the whole company. Commenting upon this technique in the novel Jones said that *The Thin Red Line* has a fly's eye viewpoint. A fly eye is composed of hundred little cylinders and the whole viewpoint is similar, so that in the same line or paragraph the viewpoint will change from man to man (Karl, 80). Jones's point of view in the novel resembles a cubist painting which offers a multidimensional perspective to the viewer, presenting manifold facets of the same object. The character Witt in the novel is a reincarnation of Prewitt and like him comes from Kentucky and across the entire Island to join the Charlie Company, which he loves with almost dog-like loyalty. This, despite the fact that Witt has been transferred out to another outfit called Cannon Company. The character of Mad Welsh is Warden reincarnated, he is a competent soldier but has almost lost his sanity, and his efficiency is fuelled by alcohol. Mess Sergeant Storm, the reincarnation of Stark from the earlier novel appears as a more positive character in the novel. Nevertheless Jones does not subject these characters to an in-depth analysis because ultimately they are reduced to a non-entity and become 'automatons' or 'instruments' of the war.

Writing about *The Thin Red Line* in his book *Cannibals and Christians* Norman Mailer expressed the opinion that the novel was so broad and true a picture of combat that it could be used as a textbook at the Infantry school. Mailer was also of the view that Jones's intention was not to create 'characters' but the feel of combat, and the psyche of men involved in warfare. In this novel Jones reveals the further evolution of the soldier when in a face-to-face confrontation with a foreign military enemy he is forced to suppress his sense of self. The romantic idealism and individualism of Prewitt, admirable though it may be has no place in a situation where group co-operation is essential to minimizing casualties. Such combat is the situation for which Warden was attempting to prepare himself in *From Here to Eternity*. The characters in the present novel have largely succeeded in sacrificing their sense of self to the welfare of C-for-Charlie Company. Such sacrifice is almost never the result of abstract loyalty or idealism rather it is an instinctive realization that whatever safety is possible in combat lies in the smooth functioning of the company. Only two characters, Witt and Welsh exhibit signs of loyalty towards their unit. However, this loyalty is only for the Company and not for the country. The kind of brutal hand-to-hand combat, which Jones depicted in the novel, involves the senseless, anonymous death, the portrayal of which is Jones's central concern. Maxwell Geismar is of the opinion that the main character of *The Thin Red Line* is really Charlie Company. Some of its enlisted men die and its officers are constantly changing, but the company continues to exist (Geismar, 40). Stephen Crane in his *The Red Badge of Courage*, depicting a similar kind of anonymity hit upon the device of referring to his characters as 'the youth', the 'tall soldier' and 'the loud soldier'.

The title which was taken from a quotation by Rudyard Kipling has several resonances: The line formed by soldiers when forced by large number of attackers is the traditional 'thin red line' where they have to defend themselves against the enemy. There is also an old mid western saying that "there's only a thin red line between the sane and the mad" and this becomes a conception of considerable significance in combat. There is also a potential third meaning, the thin red line of blood that trails from the dying and the dead. In a perceptive essay, Paulette Michell Michot argues that the novel is organized around the concept of crossing a line: "between the human and the animal, between reason and sensibility on the one side, and brutality and morbid cruelty on the other" (Michot, 15).

The success of a nation at war depends upon the love of the country that its institutions instill in its citizens from an early age. A byproduct of this love is to cultivate in each person a sense of duty to fight in order to protect the state when it is endangered. Consequently, all the citizens exert social pressure on one another to do their duty, and to refuse is virtually unthinkable because the self-esteem of the modern individual is so tightly bound to the opinions of others. In *The Thin Red Line* however Jones echoing the belief of other novelists unequivocally declares that there are no brave or noble causes left to fight for in modern society and patriotism and devotion to one's country is mere cant. He demystifies the concept of the brave American 'man' who knows no fear and like Hemingway's tough male heroes shows grace under pressure in every eventuality including death. This notion of 'masculinity' is not confined to the American nation alone. In every country and society throughout their childhood little boys are subject to social conditioning to live up to a role that tells them that being a man means being brave, even fearless in the face of any threatening presence. However, Jones shatters the myth of the rugged American soldier by stripping away heroism from war revealing that contrary to popular belief, a soldier is terribly afraid of combat like all ordinary human beings and effectively shatters the legend of the brave soldier created by films and the media.

The author demythologizes the glory of war through the character of Corporal Fife who had joined the army with grand illusions about killing and defeating the cruel 'Japs'. Before witnessing combat Fife like Stephen Crane's hero Henry Fleming had imagined war to be heroic and gallant but when he arrives on the Island, he discovers that all his fellow soldiers are terrified of the enemy. Initially Fife tries to lecture them on concepts such as patriotism and devotion to one's country but after witnessing the vicious battle for the target known as 'Giant Boiled Shrimp', Fife is exposed to the terrible jungle warfare and realizes that he too is mortally afraid of being killed in battle. Unable to wear the mask of heroism any longer, Fife openly admits that he is an 'honest coward'. His grand illusions shattered, he minutely analyzes war and wonders about the concept of valour in war:

> "This was war? There was no superior test of strength here, no superb swordsmanship, no bellowing Viking heroism, and no expert marksmanship. This was only numbers. He was being killed for numbers." (*TRL*, 152)

Soldiers like Welsh who show 'loyalty' display this emotion only towards the Company and not the country. Welsh speaks contemptuously of such abstracts as 'politics', 'religion', 'ideas and integrity' and maintains that he believes only in 'property', declaring that human lust for territory, is what controls governments and inspires wars. Welsh is of the opinion that World War II is a large scale, massive confrontation in human history over property and believes that democracy and freedom are principles that had no place in the battleground.

As has been mentioned the 'animalism' of human beings is present in all the three novels but in *The Thin Red Line* the author projects this bestiality rather forcefully. Just before going into the struggle for the 'Dancing Elephant', the company learns of the fate of two American soldiers who after being captured by the Japanese were tortured to death and then their bodies were brutally mutilated. Such news confirms the collective belief of Charlie Company that they will confront a subhuman enemy, which can only be fought on a level of primitive barbarity. The 'animalism' of man is demonstrated during a scene where drunken men of the Charlie Company after the battle of the target known as Elephant Slug get into a brawl amongst themselves and baying like 'wolves' stagger to the tent of their new Company commander to tell him how much they hate him. There is no saintliness here, no brotherhood, no co-operative utopia only debasement and degradation.

The character of Witt in *The Thin Red Line* is a reincarnation of Prewitt reduced to an almost animal level. Peter Aichinger argues, "in Witt the human elements have disappeared; he is practically an idiot, neither physically nor morally attractive" (Aichinger, 31). Aichinger contends that this signals Jones's repudiation of the romanticism of Prewitt because "Prewitt's individualism becomes Witt's perversity and Prewitt's loyalty to his private code of conduct becomes Witt's 'goddamed, stupid Kentucky code'". In the novel his idealism for all the 'underdogs' has disappeared and so has his association with art. What is left is the stubborn 'Bolshevik' with a self-destructive loyalty to his Company. Witt is now with the Canon Company but keeps coming back to the Charlie Company. Whenever the fighting becomes especially deadly, he reappears in the midst of his old outfit and volunteers for the most dangerous patrols. Witt is what Prewitt might have been had he lived to see combat. However, towards the end of the novel, Witt is reassigned to his former Company and embarks with them towards New Georgia to fight another battle.

To conclude in *The Thin Red Line* Jones reveals the further evolution of a soldier through his experience in combat. The end of the novel sees C-for-Charlie Company embarking for New Georgia. The Company has survived to fight again but very few of its old members have survived and it now consists of a boatload of new recruits led by a handful of veterans. Nonetheless, all the historical accounts will speak of C-for-Charlie as one ongoing, continuous entity. Mess Sergant Storm comes to the conclusion that under these circumstances the individual depersonalized by combat had become 'a tool with its serial number of manufacture stamped right on it'. Even Nature, in the form of the jungle, knows the insignificance of the individual—"Almost invisible in the rain, it loomed there, alien, supremely confident, making them aware of it even when they could not see it, a fact of nature like a mountain or an ocean and equally as ominous to the human ego" (*TRL*, 480). Finally, the former Company commander, Captain Stein, contemplating upon the situation of the men realizes:

> "Some men would survive, but no one individual man could survive. It was a discrepancy in methods of counting. The whole thing was too vast, too complicated, too technological for any one individual man to count in it. Only collections of men counted, only communities of men, only numbers of men." (*TRL*, 485).

As they are marching away from the Island the members of the Company pass a boy perched on a wrecked Japanese barge, eating an apple. They pass on and 'mad' Welsh chuckles and declares that he doesn't need apples because he has his gin. Welsh knows that even if most of the men survive New Georgia, there will be many more Islands to conquer. The boy eating the apple does not have such knowledge, nor do the rest of the Charlie Company. Maxwell Geismar is of the view that the novel ends on a powerful note and the whole impact of *The Thin Red Line* is that the C-for-Charlie Company must go back into the battle line again and the whole unbearable and monstrous ordeal must be undergone once more.

The symbolism in the last scene is subtly effective. What Welsh comprehends goes beyond good and evil and perhaps beyond the possibility of communication to others. The last line of the novel would seem to state the impossibility of communicating such bitter wisdom:

> "One day one of their number would write a book about all this, but none of them would write a book about all this, but none of them would believe it, because none of them would remember it that way." (*TRL*, 495).

Whistle: The Disintegration of a Soldier

James Jones's last novel in the trilogy deals with the 'disintegration' of the soldier. The soldier having lost his individual identity due to the regimentation and totalitarianism of the army and the horrifying experiences of combat cannot find his true self after he is evacuated from the organization. Alienation, anxiety and depression are the dominant themes of this novel. The soldiers who return from the war find that they have come back to a 'changed' world, a world to which they cannot adjust. *Whistle* does not match up to the narrative power of Jones's earlier novels and received a barrage of criticism when it was published with critics like Peter Prescott and Thomas Edwards calling it a very badly written book, with too much emphasis on sex. John Aldrige however published an extremely perceptive analysis of the novel in *The New York Times*, Book Review saying that *Whistle* made clear 'the developing theme of the trilogy as a whole' and also focused on soldiers coming home from battlefields who had to wage a special kind of war for survival in a society that had undergone a major transformation in the post war period (Aldridge, 30-31).

In *Whistle* Jones explains that men who have been trained to kill and accept the inevitability of their own deaths and who have seen humanity at its worst, in its animal form simply cannot come home with the innocence they once possessed.

However, the civilians cannot comprehend this fact, and a barrier grows up between the returning soldiers and the civilians. Jones who faced a similar difficulty after returning home from war makes a statement about this increasing gap between those who have been a witness to a world conflagration and those who stayed at home. In his journal *World War II* he says that the civilians cannot comprehend that they have a lot of dead men around them, dead men who are walking around and breathing. *Whistle* focuses on four casualties of the same infantry company that had fought in Guadalcanal and New Georgia. The four have been shipped home towards the end of the war as evacuees with grievous injuries. Three of the four represent characterizations begun in *From Here to Eternity* and continued in *The Thin Red Line* and *Whistle*: "In *Whistle* Welsh becomes Mart Winch, Witt becomes Bobby Prell, Storm becomes John Strange" (*Whistle*, ii). The characters are not the same people any more, hence the change in names. The fourth character, Marion Landers seems a refinement of Fife in *The Thin Red Line*.

The novel tells the story of Mart Winch and three men of his Company Landers, Prell and Strange who are shipped back to the United States wounded, only to find that after their discharge from the army, their lives have become meaningless and purposeless. They have been away for many years fighting the Japanese in the Pacific and in their absence, America has changed radically and now they feel alienated from its present environment. The experience of these soldiers is similar to the one, which Jones had when he returned to his country after being evacuated from the army due to a head wound. Writing about soldiers returning from war, Jones said that it was a different America altogether from the one so many of them had left before the war.

The soldiers have not only been depersonalized after having served in the army but the endless combat has also taken a toll on their nerves, leaving them completely shattered. As the wounded soldiers return home they find themselves on the verge of a collapse. Winch, who is facing death by congestive heart failure, finds a purpose in his life when he decides to protect the lives of the other three men of his former Company. Jones's task is similar to that of his protagonist; for thirty years he has written about soldiers in combat, carrying his characters from one novel to another and like Winch he finds it difficult to let go.

The author beautifully plots the tragic situation of Winch who must not only save the lives of his men but also their psyche and yet for various reasons cannot reveal how much he is doing for them. He forces Prell, for example, to hate him because he knows that only a worthy antagonist will stir up the last reserve of energy that Prell needs to fight in order to save his badly wounded legs. Prell fights successfully against the figment of Winch's enmity but after having won the Congressional medal for bravery, he becomes a 'pin up boy' for war bond rallies, ultimately dying during a brawl in a low class bar.

Landers the cynical clerk of Winch's former Company finds some purpose in his life when he joins another Company of the army (stationed away from the battlefield) and straightens out the paperwork of this Company. However his sense of purpose is defeated when the Lieutenant of this Company is transferred due to anti-Semitic prejudices. Lander's protests are futile and after being saved from a court martial by Winch, Landers commits suicide. Winch's purpose in life disappears and he suffers a breakdown. The novel ends with the last of the four men Strange, slipping overboard to drown in the sea.

The men who have lost their identity during combat find the change in American society deeply disturbing. The soldiers who had spent years in the army and had come to regard the organization as their family feel lost. The aspect of the new America, which deeply disturbs them, is the economic affluence produced by the war and the accompanying drastic change in morality. James Giles is of the opinion that while Jones is quite successful in conveying their outrage at wartime profiteering but his attempt to depict their dismay at changing sexual mores is forced and unconvincing and he works very hard to demonstrate that the respectable Puritanism in which they grew up is largely to blame for this. Thus, alienation, anxiety and depression are the dominant themes of this novel as the author delineates the growing alienation of his characters from the world around them.

To begin with, C-for-Charlie Company's former clerk Lander's alienation leads to his destruction. Jones reveals through a series of flashbacks that Landers sense of dislocation began during the battle of Guadalcanal when he felt irrevocably estranged from the human race, which could engage in such barbarity. Landers is also tormented by a sense of guilt involving another episode in the war, when he drank water from his canteen while several starving and thirsty men of his Company looked at him with 'no envy'. Despite their lack of resentment, Landers felt that he had sinned by drinking water in their presence. Once the Company clerk who had always found it difficult to build up permanent relationships returns to America, his sense of segregation increases and he feels 'isolated' and lonely among wounded fellow soldiers at the army hospital. Unable to find friends among his comrades, Landers turns to his family for relief, but to no avail. His return to Indiana where his family is socially prominent is disastrous as Landers feuds with his father who wants to 'show him off' as a war hero. He drinks heavily at the local club and then makes a speech to the new draftees regarding war and debunking its glory:

> "I can't in honesty tell you that you will be fighting for freedom, and God, and your country.... In combat you don't think about any of that. But I can assure you that you will be fighting for your life.... I think that's a good thing to fight for." (*Whistle*, 166)

Landers cuts off all ties from his family and in desperation turns to women but finds no relief in these relationships either. Feeling deeply frustrated, he finds an uncontrollable 'red rage' building up inside him, which gets him involved in fistfights with other soldiers. Ultimately, Landers quarrels with a wounded soldier, has a verbal confrontation with the administrative chief and goes AWOL (Absent without official leave) for five days. After being acquitted in a court martial (primarily due to Winch's efforts), Landers unable to find peace, commits suicide.

The next character in the novel is Mess Sergeant John Strange and Jones reveals that his destruction occurs primarily because he has built a wall around himself and lives in isolation, keeping his emotions bottled up inside him. Furthermore, Strange feels estranged from American society because he fails to adjust to the prevailing sexual mores and comes to regard women as 'enemy'. Strange's isolation begins when he discovers that his wife is being unfaithful to him and forms a relationship with a woman named Francis Highsmith. This relationship fails and an embittered Strange asks for a transfer to another Company, thereby expressing a desire to go back to the warfront. However, as he is being shipped back he commits suicide by deliberately slipping overboard. Jones describes his action thus: "As he hit the water he himself is shocked by what he has done. It was such a sudden thing that he didn't know he was going to do it" (*Whistle*, 456).

Prell's disintegration is perhaps the most tragic in the novel. Badly injured during the war, Prell faces a possible amputation and a future where he would be confined to a wheelchair. However, the brave soldier stubbornly refuses to have his legs cut off and when he is offered a Medal of Honour for heroism in war, he refuses arguing that he would much rather retain his legs. Prell suffers from a sense of guilt triggered by an episode during the war.

During a campaign in New Georgia, he had stumbled upon an enemy troop concentration and spotted General Sasaki, the Japanese commander of the New Georgia operation. As Prell tried to kill him something went wrong, his men were ambushed and the Japanese opened fire during which Prell was wounded and two of his men killed. Prell now feels guilty about the way his men died and how the other men risked their lives and carried him on a stretcher to safety. His guilt is further exacerbated when he gets a Medal of Honour.

Prell decides to fight back to save his legs and miraculously begins to recover. Ironically, the Medal of Honour contributes significantly to his destruction as after his recovery, Prell is made a celebrity and compelled to sell 'war bonds'. He impregnates a nurse Della Mae Kinkaid and is forced to marry her, but soon discovers that the marriage was deliberately planned because Della wished to 'cash in' on Prell's celebrity status. Further, Prell is disgusted by the American ethos of attempting to make money during a situation like war. His wounds and experiences during war are turned into a profit-making venture by greedy human beings and disgusted by his new role as a war hero his sense of alienation reaches its peak. Furthermore, after his recovery he has nothing to fight for and the ultimate blow is struck when he learns of Landers and Strange's death. Disillusioned and shattered Prell is left with nothing but a reputation as 'war hero' and a celebrity bond salesman. He begins to pick up fights in dingy bars with the deliberate intention of getting killed and ultimately succeeds.

Forty-two-year old Mart Winch's disintegration begins when he starts getting isolated from his sense of self and is tormented by a 'persistent sense of another him'. Jones indicates that Winch is losing his sanity as he is plagued by recurrent nightmares about the war where he is always on a hill in Guadalcanal looking down at his men trapped by Japanese fire, where he is shouting "Get them out of there.... They're bracketing in on them! Get them out of there!" (*Whistle*, 294).

Because of his mental and physical ill health Winch feels too weak to be everyone else's source of strength yet he tries to save them as he feels it is the only way to maintain his sanity. Like the other men, he too has a series of failed relationships and is betrayed by his wife who abandons him for another man. Winch tries his utmost to save Landers, Prell and Strange from destruction but when this fails his mental collapse becomes imminent.

Like many of his contemporaries Jones conceived all the three novels in Naturalistic terms, sympathetic towards the marginalized soldier who suffers terribly at the hands of the officers in the army who are symbolic of the bourgeois middle class. The army is a metaphor for the capitalist society in the novel. Prewitt becomes a spokesperson for Jones's ideology as the author informs his readers that Prewitt was trapped in an environment, which stripped away his dignity, and self-respect and from where there were only two possible escape routes; the army which ironically destroys and music which becomes a symbol of beauty in his otherwise sordid life. Despite the fact that he does not have any ideological beliefs Prewitt shows senstivity towards his fellow sufferers. He shows sympathy towards the Communists in Spain who fought the Spanish Civil War against their oppressive rulers but has no feelings for the Russian Communists because they are dictators who resorted to exploitation of their people. It is ultimately his sympathy for the underdog, which makes him murder Fatso Judson who becomes a symbol of cruelty and oppression. Although Milt Warden, the other character in the novel does not display overt sympathy for the underdog, his hatred of the bourgeoisie middle class and commiseration for Prewitt makes him a champion of the proletarian soldier. Warden's stubborn refusal to become an officer stems from his deep distrust of the middle class and he condemns them acrimoniously in a speech: "Who do you think was put Hitler up? The workers? No it was the same middle class. Who do you think gave the Communists Russia? The peasants? No, the Commisars. That same goddamn middleclass" (*Eternity*, 621-22).

In novels like *The Thin Red Line* Jones's Naturalism becomes evident through his realistic portrayal of battle scenes. As a part of this philosophy, Jones demonstrates the role played by Nature in the novel. The vast forests of Guadalcanal prove to be a major adversary for the hapless soldiers who often fall prey to the jungle and its mysterious ways. The long march through thick foliage 'where no sunbeam pries' is tortuous for the men who have never had such close contact with Nature at its worst. The jungle becomes a symbol of primitivism and cannibalism. In *Whistle* Jones reveals how the soldier is hopelessly trapped by his circumstances and environment. The characters in the novel who return from war find that they do not belong and ultimately kill themselves.

A discussion of Jones's novel would be incomplete without a comment on his 'tough' writing. Critics argue that Jones's success is limited to a particular milieu and like Hemingway he is a 'tough' 'male' writer who does not portray, rather cannot portray female characters sympathetically. Masculine interests, attitudes and values govern this world. No woman can step into this world without immediately altering its character. Milton Virost is of the view that:

> "Jones acquired the reputation of being a man's writer, preoccupied with men's urges, men's morality, men's hang ups. Almost obsessively, Jones explores the nature of virility. His measure of a man seems all but primordial: The ability to withstand pain, the response to danger.... Jones's people move in a world of violence, where life tends to be a brutalizing experience." (Virost, 253)

Alfred Kazin believes that in Jones's world, 'maleness' becomes an aggressive need to retain the individual's sanity. However, this brutal world of male containment is tragic as it is plagued by unredeemed violence and aggression. Despite a strain of 'toughness' in his work, author's writing is extremely poignant and gentle in many places and while it is the 'he man' Jones who is superficially the more visible, it is the second who is the more important. Jones himself said during an interview:

> "I've come to consider bravery as just about the most pernicious of virtues. Bravery is a horrible thing. The human race has left it over from the animal world and we can't get rid of it." (*Aldrich*, 47)

Although Jones was primarily a Naturalist, some critics notice beginnings of rudimentary Existentialism in his novels. Critics Peter G. Jones and David Stevenson believe that novels like *From Here to Eternity* exhibit signs of this philosophy as its protagonist Prewitt is desperate to find some meaning and order in the totalitarian and absurd world of the army. Peter G. Jones is of the view that *From Here to Eternity* can be viewed as a Bildungsroman or the novel of education where the hero Prewitt (while on a quest to find meaning) learns about making 'right choices'. In making these choices and taking the right decision Prewitt adopts what can be called an existential stand, accomplishing an act of Sartrean good faith because his sense of fair play does not allow him to accept injustice. The idealistic soldier's refusal to compromise with his ethics is termed by Warden as pure stubbornness, but to Prewitt, his actions are 'right' and therefore, he would stand by them even if the consequences were terrible.

There are Existential overtones in *The Thin Red Line* as well. In this novel Jones brutally strips away all illusions, about the individual's inherent dignity and being and the individual in combat disappears into the bureaucratic 'collective' becoming a 'part' of the war machine. In the ferocity of war, existence is viewed as a grotesque dance with death in a senseless and meaningless universe. In his novels Jones portrays this world in both Naturalistic and faintly Existential terms. Thus, Jones's war novels have much in common with other twentieth-century war novels like John Hawkes *The Cannibal* or Joseph Heller's *Catch 22* in that they explore the fate of the individual in the modern world which has become meaningless, absurd increasingly mechanical and inhuman.

In conclusion, Jones's trilogy is a tribute to all the soldiers who fought the Second Great War. In *Whistle*, the author declares that his novels have been dedicated to:

> "Every man who served in the US Armed Forces in World War II—whether he survived or not; whether he made fortune serving or not; whether he fought or not; whether he did time or not; whether he went crazy, or didn't." (*Whistle*, i)

Norman Mailer: *The Naked and the Dead*

3

Norman Mailer's novel *The Naked and the Dead* published in 1948 is one of the most successful novels about World War II. The novel brought Mailer stupendous success and unnerving acclaim although James Jones's *From Here to Eternity* gave it tough competition and Mailer himself was of the view that Jones's work of fiction was better than his own. Mailer has been a controversy-courting writer, his works have always been a subject of debate and his first novel was no exception. By and large it was praised and was highly appreciated. Alfred Kazin called it 'the best book on World War II' (Kazin, 78) while John Aldridge called Mailer 'the best literary mind of the war generation' (Aldridge, 258). Walter B. Rideout looked upon the novel as positive and hopeful rather than negative and pessimistic (Rideout, 253) and Chester Eisinger opined that *The Naked and the Dead* was the best novel of ideas written in America (Eisinger, 33). However, the novel received its share of criticism as well. Gore Vidal called it 'a clever, admirably executed fake' (Vidal, 13) and Marvin Mudrick expressed the view that it is everything but a novel about the war in the Pacific. "It is full of bits of writing that fit neatly into pigeon holes, it is fine writing about death and about America as the melting pot" (Mudrick, 364). Kingsley Widmer was of the view that Mailer was not a good novelist and that nothing he has written may be called major or useful (Widmer, 15). These opinions about *The Naked and the Dead* are interesting because they put the novel in perspective.

Mailer wrote in *The Advertisements for Myself* that he had joined the army with the idea that when he came out he would write a novel about the war. While a sense of shock and peril gripped the nation after the attack on Pearl Harbour on December 7, 1941, Mailer spent two days worrying whether his 'great war' novel should be written about Europe or the Pacific. He initially decided on Europe, but soon realized that Europe was an 'old literary territory' and writers like Hemingway and E.E. Cummings had written about the European war already. Moreover, some of these writers had lived in Europe for many years as expatriates and were familiar with the culture of the Continent. Mailer however, had no sense of the culture or past of Europe and hence would not be able to write a successful European war novel. Therefore, he decided to document a history of war in the Pacific theatre. Further, he wanted to write a realistic novel, based on personal experience, as it would not have been possible for him to work up his experience in the library as Stephen Crane did for his *The Red Badge of Courage.* Therefore he got himself drafted in the army in 1941, but was initially offered the desk job of a clerk which he refused because as a writer, he wanted the knowledge of real combat. Ultimately, Mailer served as a rifleman in a reconnaissance platoon in the Pacific, witnessed brutal hand-to-hand combat and exposed himself to the raw material of his novel, all the time testing, himself to discover, if as a young intellectual he had the courage and endurance for war.

The integrity of his ego and the validation of his romantic attitude towards experience were at stake in this testing. Both were vital to Mailer in the writing of *The Naked and the Dead*, for the novel was to rise from his certified capacities as a fighting man. Mailer already had the title of the novel in his mind because he had written a play about an insane asylum called *The Naked and the Dead*. After he was discharged from the army Mailer initially wrote a short story based on the Second Great War. The story entitled *A Calculus at Heaven* is set in the Pacific just as *The Naked and the Dead* was to be. It is also predictive of the novel in style, form and incident as it is in the mode of Dos Passos, full of flashbacks into the prewar lives of the various characters, who are a part of the doomed action on an Island named Tinde. Each of the characters in the story symbolize different enclaves of American Society and comprise of an Irish Priest Father Mceary, an Italian named Da Lucci, an American Indian Sergeant Rice, and a Jew from New Jersey named Wexler. All these characters have social and other similarities to characters in the novel and Wexler undertakes an expedition that is similar to the one undertaken by Sergeant Martinez in *The Naked and the Dead.* The most important character in the short story however, is Captain Brown Hillard, the son of an army Colonel and a graduate of Yale University. Hillard closely resembles Lieutenant Hearn in *The Naked and the Dead.*

Technically, Mailer emulates the Naturalistic tradition of Farell, Hemingway, Dreisier and especially Dos Passos, and has admitted as much in an interview to the Paris Review. But Mailer's novel moves beyond the influence of these writers and outlines the ideas, values and changes in consciousness of a new generation that emerged after World War II. Mailer's novel is political in nature and he writes as a soldier from the ranks, from a shrewd observation of human beings involved in brutal combat. In *The Naked and the Dead*, the author warns his readers against the latent dangers of war and the long-term impact of conflict rather than dramatizing and sensationalizing the suffering of soldiers although he does touch upon these themes briefly. The novel is based on an ideological debate and raises an important question—would war lead to an establishment of totalitarianism in American society or would the liberal democratic spirit of the country survive after the war? However, despite the fact that the novel's central theme is an ideological conflict there appears to be an all-pervasive, drastically accelerated sense of time in *The Naked and the Dead* as time is always running out on the soldiers and death hotly pursues them.

The action of the novel is set on the fictitious Island of Anopopei, the main focus being the Intelligence and Reconnaissance (I&R) Platoon. The regiment of troops is under the command of the diabolical General Cummings who has his own ideas regarding war and democracy. The regiment is sent to the Island to recapture it from the Japanese. Mailer introduces us to the cast of characters Croft, Wilson, Red Valsen, Stanley, victims who joined the army to escape the oppressive, exploitative American society.

On the night before their arrival the atmosphere on the troop ship is tense as the members of Sergeant Croft's I and R squad alternate between boredom, and anxiety. Two soldiers, Wilson and Gallagher play a desultory game of poker with the Sergeant while Red Valsen wanders sleeplessly around the deck as Sergeant Brown talks to Stanley, an ambitious young G.I. (Government Issue) anxious for promotion, and Sergeant Julio Martinez the squad's Mexican scout, lies in his bunk sweating with fear. Shortly before dawn, the naval bombardment of the Island begins. Croft, a tough professional soldier who delights in combat and killing briefs his men and leads them into the landing vessels.

During the next few days, the troops push forward into the interior of Anopopei. The jungle which continually separates the various companies, poses greater problems than the Japanese, as General Cummings conducts the advance in a leisurely fashion, building roads and creating supply lines as he goes, for he realizes that the Japanese are reserving their strength for a later battle. Croft, who is working on a beach detail, is angered at the poor quality of new men added to his squad, Wyman, Roth and Goldstein who are all nervous and inexperienced soldiers. In the officers' mess Lieutenant Hearn, a liberal minded young Harvard graduate is disgusted by the coarseness and conservatism of his fellow officers Hobart, Dalleson and Conn, he insults Conn and is saved from an embarrassing incident by the intervention of Cummings. By now, the American soldiers are close to the Japanese general Toyaku's lines. During a heavy rainstorm, the Japanese mount a mortar attack and Cummings counters this with his usual dexterity. Croft's squad is sent into action, hauling heavy guns along slippery roads and through dense undergrowth. They meet Japanese troops near a river and Croft with his delight in killing, marshals his men into repelling the attack.

The author draws the reader's attention towards Hearn and shows that despite his guilt and uneasiness in the role of an officer, Hearn is drawn into an increasingly intimate relationship with Cummings as he is attracted by his superior's intelligence. However, he feels repelled by his cold and arrogant conservatism. After the successful countering of the Japanese attack the American advance comes to a grinding halt, and this annoys Cummings who vents his frustration by bullying and humiliating his former favourite Hearn. At last, the General works out a new strategy: he would send a reconnaissance patrol around the south side of the Island to attack the enemy from behind, while a major frontal assault would be initiated. Croft's squad is chosen for the task and Hearn is put in command. Hearn has mixed feelings, pleasure at being away from Cummings, with whom he has had several altercations in the past regarding ideologies and the purpose of war (Cummings hated rebellion and Hearn had rebelled against Cummings) and anxious regarding the mission and the dangers involved. Hearn and Croft jostle for effective command over the squad. On the second day of the mission, they start out already enervated by the heat but quickly fall into a Japanese ambush. In confusion, they retreat without realizing that a member of the platoon, Wilson has been left behind wounded. Croft deputes Brown, Ridges, Stanley and Goldstein to rescue him. Hearn feels that the mission should be abandoned but Croft is in favour of continuing. They send Martinez out during the night to look for Japanese patrol but although the scout observes a large number of the enemy (indeed he has to kill a Japanese soldier) Croft persuades him to conceal this information from Hearn. When the squad advances the next morning Hearn is killed by a Japanese sniper, actually it is Croft who tricks him into getting killed. Against growing protests, Croft insists that the squad continue to advance and climb the formidable Mount Anaka, literally forcing the men to scale the difficult terrain. The men hate the mountain and encounter several difficulties while climbing it, the group with Wilson meets with similar difficulties as Stanley and Brown collapse with fatigue, leaving Ridges and Goldstein to carry the wounded man.

The action shifts towards General Cummings who has temporarily left the Island to get naval support for his frontal attack. In his absence, the mediocre Major Dalleson launches an attack on the Japanese and finding that this assault is successful, completes the operation before Cummings' return. In the jubilation of the victory the fate of Croft's squad is forgotten. Wilson dies and his body is washed away in the sea. Ridges and Goldstein, once antagonistic, but now made intimate by their mutual ordeal, stumble on the shore to await the boat, which will collect them. Croft still tries to get his squad to push ahead and climb the formidable Mt Anaka. Ironically, the platoon abandons the patrol not due to an attack by the Japanese but when they stumble into a hornet's nest and retreat in panic. Croft realizes that he cannot persuade the men to return and allows them to make their way to the beach, where the navy picks them up. Cummings is enraged by the fact that the credit of the victory over the Japanese should go to a second-rate officer like Major Dalleson, he is a little shocked by Hearn's death but ultimately starts assessing the profit and loss of the campaign.

Structurally the novel is well made. Mailer said that it was written mechanically, and was the work of a young engineer. Mailer structured the novel not only to outline the story of armed conflict on the fictitious Island of Anopopei but also the stories of each of the main characters involved in the struggle. He often breaks his narrative with flashbacks or 'Time Machine' segments delving into the past history of characters like Roth, Wilson, Red Valsen, Croft, Stanley and others. These sections are an integral part of the overall structure of the novel as they provide important background information about these characters.

Peter G. Jones is of the opinion that Mailer's novel is structured according to a well-controlled order and rhythm. Part one titled 'Wave' is a brief prologue, which sets the locale, launches the action, and introduces the reader to the cast of characters, the men of the Reconnaissance platoon. The title of this section is significant. The 'wave' refers to the murmuring protest of the soldiers against their situation. Just as the waves murmur against the seashore the soldiers too covertly raise their voice against the sordid life in the hostile jungles but to no avail. The war too is like a wave whipped up somewhere offshore gathering amplitude and direction crashing upon a beach and receding once again. In this ebb and flow of meaningless warfare the only fact is death and confronted by that fact man is naked. The first death of the novel occurs in this section as Hennessey gets swept up by the wave of violence, and gets killed during bombardment.

Part two 'Argil and the Mold' focuses on General Cummings as the totalitarian, power hungry General tries to 'mould' the clay like soldiers into following the system of the army. The soldiers are clay because they are malleable and can be moulded in accordance with the General's desires and his strategy for fighting the war. Part three of the novel titled 'Plant and Phantom' deals with I&R Platoon's disastrous mission. Hearn's death is a shocking event in this section and Croft's love for violence establishes him as an inhuman creature devoid of any emotions. Part four of the novel 'Wake' is a very brief epilogue where Cummings reviews the debacle of the patrol that was to have provided the foundation for his rise to power and resolves to try another scheme and if this too failed he would obtain clout through politics.

Chester Eisinger is of the opinion that the ideological conflict in the novel provides a structural principle. It offers a scheme by which the readers may arrange the characters in a particular order and understand their relationship with one another. Thus, Lieutenant Hearn and Red Valsen represent liberalism and anti-authoritarianism while General Cummings and Sergeant Croft represent militarism and fascism. From much of this conflict stems the action, and the fate of the characters depends on the resolution of this conflict. However, Eisinger is of the view that the novel is not tautly conceived and the Time Machine sections or intercalary chapters that have been used by Mailer to flashback into the lives of his characters before the war are an aberration that interrupts the flow of the narrative.

In *The Naked and the Dead* Mailer writes about war, combat and the experiences of a soldier, highlighting the waste and degradation caused by an armed conflict. However, Mailer's novel is much more than a story about military tactics and suffering of soldiers during combat. It moves beyond these clichés and looks upon war as a form of social organization and an extension of contemporary American society, which was perceived by Mailer as despotic, tyrannical and exploitative. World War I was widely viewed by post-war authors as a catastrophe and a breakdown of civilization. On the other hand, the important novelists of World War II (and this is one of the important distinctions between them) have tended to see it as a natural outgrowth of modern civilization and culture, not as an aberration and this view is implicit in *The Naked and the Dead* as well. The novel thus is a critique of the American culture of abundance and materialism, which leads to the alienation of the individual. This idea finds a trenchant expression in the novel and the author displays his Leftist leanings when he puts forth his views. The characters in the novel are victims of the Great Depression and the shattering of the American Dream, these soldiers are 'damaged material' who are as pathetic in South Boston, San Antonio and Brooklyn as they are in the army.

In the Time Machine sections of the novel Mailer criticizes America and explains that the actions and attitudes of soldiers in the army is a product of social determinism at home. One of the earliest critics of the novel, John W. Aldridge, sets the tone for many to follow when he writes that Mailer's 'Time Machine' portraits show us that the lives of the men were already purposeless and futile before the war and this situation has merely been exacerbated by the conflict. The overall effect of the contrast between the portraits from the past and the present wartime scenes is to intensify the novel's mood of anomie, hopelessness, and meaninglessness. Hemingway, Cummings, and even Dos Passos in his 'Left' days never saw war as the inevitable extension of American civilization.

Among the psychological problems created by society, the most obvious is racial and other types of discrimination. In these inter-chapters or the Time Machine sections the readers are presented with grim vignettes of American lives where in a dominantly Anglo-Saxon, White Protestant culture all minority groups bear the special psychic burden of being the 'outsider' or the 'other'. The cross section of soldiers, who make up the characters of the novel, are carefully selected. Gallagher is a frustrated and an inarticulate product of lower middle class Boston Irish culture and his world is a world of dreariness, despondency and dissipation. Mailer describes his life thus:

> "In South Boston and Dorchester the gray wooden houses parade for miles in a file of drabness and desolation and waste...there are no Jews or Italians or Irish—their features have blurred in an anonymous mortar which has rendered them homogeneous and dusty. They all talk with the same depressing, harsh and arid tongue." (*The Naked and the Dead*, 282)

Gallagher has faced excruciating poverty and is extremely frustrated at being a failure in life. He ultimately turns to the pseudo satisfaction of native fascism (he hates Jews) in order to compensate for the inadequacies of his own life. On the other hand another soldier of Mailer's platoon Joey Goldstein is a product of lower middle class Brooklyn Jewish culture, who feels alienated from the Christian mainstream of American life and is victimized by sexual insecurities. Goldstein is a high school and welding school graduate with a wife, son, and a dream of owning his own welding shop. Mailer describes Goldstein as possessing an 'ingenuous nature,' and as a man who is 'always trusting' and who 'never became completely disheartened' despite his sordid environment.

Essentially Goldstein is active and efficient but prone to occasional fits of despondency during which he becomes almost fatalistic, asking himself, "Oh, what does it all mean? What are we born for, why do we work? You're born and then you die, is that all there is to it?... You're born and then you die" (*The Naked and the Dead*, 473). Furthermore, men seeming friendly one day and snubbing him the next are constantly disillusioning him. He bemoans the fact that he always has 'to be nicer than the next fellow' gradually becoming obsessed with the feeling that anti-Semitism dictates the relationships with all men. This is not simply a figment of Goldstein's imagination as he has faced great persecution in the past on account of being a Jew and encounters more prejudice when he joins the army. When he finally accepts anti-Semitism as a ruthless reality he finds his good spirits and self-confidence dissolving and feels alienated from his environment all the time and Mailer describes him as being 'lonely'. Thus, despite the fact that Goldstein inherently possesses a hopeful and a positive temperament his environment has a negative impact on his disposition. The soldier named Ridges is shown as staunch, stoical, and dependable and like everyone in the novel, his environment forms his character. Mailer reveals the essence of his life in the following passage:

"I'll tell you, Ossie," his father had said, "a man works and he toils, he puts in his good sweat tryin to pull out a livin from the land, and when all his work is done, if the good Lord sees it fitten, it's taken away in a storm" (*The Naked and the Dead*, 97). Ridges accepts his fate without questioning the will of God but often feels depressed and dejected by destiny's decree, which has caused him to be a failure. In reality however it is society that is responsible for his lack of success.

Martinez, the Mexican, wanted to be a hero but his life too becomes a saga of failed dreams. In the Time Machine section Mailer writes: "Little Mexican boys also breathe the American fables, also want to be heroes, aviators, lovers, financiers" (*The Naked and the Dead*, 65). For Martinez the American Dream shatters when he is crushed by poverty and as a poor Mexican faces great prejudice and discrimination from all quarters. This transforms him into a bitter and cynical individual and as a result he desperately wants to avenge himself by hurting white Protestant women. Polack, the Polish immigrant, has been brought up in the slums and like the others has faced excruciating poverty, while Brown has suffered tremendously due to the crassness, shallowness and dishonesty of the business world. Red Valsen has not been crushed by his surroundings, although his deprivation too has been severe but his sensitivity and insight have made him the wisest of the soldiers. These are characters that are a part of society that is plagued by failure and economic insecurities. All these men are struggling and waging a war to survive in a capitalistic world and have learnt to give up on deferred dreams and to hope instead for a minimal survival. Red Valsen knows: "you carried it alone as long as you could and then you weren't strong enough to take it any longer. You kept fighting everything and everything broke you down" (*The Naked and the Dead*, 207). Although Mailer devotes separate sections to each of these characters, they do not show any individuality as they have lost their identity in the struggle for survival. Even characters like Croft, Cummings and Hearn who display distinctiveness in the novel feel 'dispossessed from the raucous, stricken bosom of America'.

These soldiers are always in friction pushing, swearing, complaining and although this personal violence has not the slightest effect on the course of the war, the atmosphere is proof of General Cummings' dictum that the 'natural lot of the 20th century man is anxiety'. Mailer offers us war as a metaphor for much more besides just combat. In its structure and effects on man, it represents Mailer's view of the modern social order. Eisinger believes that as a critic of society in the cultural context, Mailer can be placed as the legitimate descendant of Whitman who makes his contribution both to the novelist's personality and to his novel. At Harvard, Mailer had been a socio-political radical, and as a rebel bears close resemblance to this great champion of democracy and individual freedom. Whitman sought a revolution in consciousness in his time with the ardent hope that from larger freedom would come greater spiritual and esthetic goods for man. *The Naked and the Dead* does not seem to document the romantic faith expressed by Whitman, but the paradox of the novel is that its angry denunciation of American society originates in the frustration of idealistic hopes for man in this country, it issues from a hurt love of America and of life itself.

Estranged from a society that threatens to wipe out their very existence, these men turn to the army, which appears to be a refuge away from disorder and chaos. Critics are of the opinion that there are similarities between Saul Bellow's novel *Dangling Man* and Mailer's *The Naked and the Dead*. In Bellow's novel we see the central character Joseph, an exhausted Existentialist who flees freedom and self-consciousness to embrace the regimentation of the army. However, the so-called order and discipline in the army is in reality a euphemism for totalitarianism and regimentation. In fact in Mailer's novel the army becomes a metaphor for society, as it is simply an extension of the oppressive system that men like Goldstein, Brown and Red have attempted to flee. Like the social set up of America, the army too is made up of officers from the middle classes who are exploitative, corrupt and ambitious. S.H. Hux is of the opinion that the army shown in the novel is "a paradigm of society, which in the name of historical necessity, captures and rules the life of humanity" (Hux, 183).

Thus the criticism of the army is an important idea in *The Naked and the Dead*. In castigating this institution Mailer warns his readers against the covert dangers of war. The author not only dislikes war because it is violent and life negating but also debunks combat because war is an incubator of totalitarianism and develops an insatiable hunger for power. It is war that makes the army powerful and during a conflict this establishment begins to function like a Fascist, tyrannical regime thriving on authority, dehumanizing and muzzling the individual completely. Mailer is of the opinion that the individual is caught in a trap from which he is unable to escape—the society provides him no succour and the army threatens to wipe out his individuality. The military becomes Mailer's metaphor for organized national violence and collective repression.

Power and the American obsession with it seem to have become the trademark of Mailer's thought. Therefore power and its relationship to both the individual and the state lead to his first dramatization of absolutism in American society. The novel's concerns thus extend beyond combat and America's physical activity in the Second World War to address the author's fear that with Truman's election in 1945 the United States would emerge from the backwaters of history to inherit its full share of the fascist dream. Cummings says in the novel: "America is going to absorb that Dream, it's in the business of doing that now" (*The Naked and the Dead,* 321). Mailer expresses a fear that America's obsession with power would make the country wage successive wars in future as well, as the nation would follow a policy of aggrandizement and coerce smaller countries into accepting their authority, inaugurating the era Neo Imperialism in future. Although *The Naked and the Dead* was written in 1948, Mailer's argument proved to be true as America was involved in a conflict first with Korea and then with Vietnam in the 1950s and 60s. Since the Second World War, America has been the most powerful capitalist state, achieving the status of a superpower. The overriding aim of its foreign policy has been to maintain its hegemony over the capitalist world and also developing nations. Until the demise of Stalinism in Eastern Europe and the former Soviet Union, its policy was to contain the economic influence and strategic power of its rival superpower, the USSR. At each stage it has acted to protect its global position: its economic dominance, its strategic power, and its prestige.

In order to do this, America built up the biggest military machine in history. Since 1945 it has consistently spent more on its nuclear weapons and armed forces, both in absolute terms and as a percentage of national product, than any other advanced capitalist country. Post Second World War America has always defended its economic interest with military power. Those that it has defended in the name of democracy have been ruthless dictators, those who have been crushed in the name of democracy have been movements and governments exploited by capitalists. American Neo Imperialism has always played a counter revolutionary role on the world arena ready to use its military power to intervene against any manifestation of social revolution.

Since Mailer looks upon war as an incubator of totalitarianism and the army as a despotic organization, power and control, ideas associated with combat and the tyranny of the army become important in the novel. Critic Donald Pizer contends that the major themes of *The Naked and the Dead* are the "nature of power and the nature of the self in relation to power, with the first theme dominating 'Argil and Mold' and the second 'Plant and Phantom'" (Pizer, 95). In an interesting commentary about the novel, critic Andrew Gordon points out that *power* and *control* are used more often than any other words in the novel. In fact, he says, after *power* and *control* the terms next highest in frequency of use are '*impotent rage* and *failure*' (Gordon, 61). The world of *The Naked and the Dead* is a world ruled by power and fear where General Cummings and Sergeant Croft, are the embodiment of the will to power.

Mailer believes that power hungry military Commanders like General Cummings who possess ambitions beyond the army and aspire to wield political authority pose the greatest threat to American society. Peter G. Jones is of the opinion that Cummings has been modeled after military Commanders like General S. Patton and General Douglas Macarthur, two important military leaders of the Second World War. Patton and Macarthur appear to have contributed most prominently to the literature of military figures. Stereotypes or caricatures derived from obvious facets of their reputations and public performances apparently served to polarize the thoughts of authors who may have written without specific commanders in mind, but who sought to universalize their statements on warfare and its impact on society. Jones argues "Patton's flamboyant mannerisms, his impressive record of combat command, and his uncompromising refusal to muzzle his remarks about peers and superiors imprinted his name in the American consciousness" (Jones, 71). Such military Commanders have been portrayed in the novels of James Gould Cozzen, Herman Wouk and Anton Myrer. These novelists display the Commanders' hunger for power and also express a concern voiced by historians like Arthur Schlesinger and J.A. Schumpeter that the greatest threat to American democracy comes from highly intelligent military Commanders with ambitions for wielding political power. The historians expressed a fear that after the war the reins of the government would be taken over by an elite warrior class. They cited the example of Egypt, where the armies, originally organized and motivated by conventional national motives for aggression, eventually created wars to justify their own existence and to perpetuate their own domestic supremacy. This resulted in the growth of an elite warrior class. Mailer articulates a similar fear in the novel. Power hungry maniacs like General Cummings would plunge America into continuous warfare.

The Second World War was responsible for giving rise to an ideological debate in America where some historians and political theorists were of the view that the war had transformed the country into a fascist nation while others insisted that America would continue adhering to the principles of democracy and liberalism. In consonance with these current ideas the novel is organized around an ideological debate, which is its central conflict. This ideological war thus forms an important part of the novel. Cummings believes that American foreign policy after the war would be very different from what it was before the war: "After the war, our foreign policy is going to be far more naked we are no longer going to cover our eyes with our left hand, while our right is extending an imperialist paw" (*The Naked and the Dead,* 338-39). As has been mentioned in the section on the structure of the novel, the characters in the novel too are drawn in ideological terms. The central concern in the novel lies in the conflict between the liberal Leftist Lieutenant Hearn and the Fascist General Cummings. Sergeant Croft and General Cummings correspond to militarism, totalitarianism and fascism while Hearn, Red and to a certain extent Roth represents liberalism, Marxism and anti-authoritarianism. The suffering men in Croft's platoon who endure unspeakable torments as they struggle through the swamp and the jungle on Cumming's order, and stumble mindlessly in the Sergeant's footsteps, as he pits himself against the unscalable height of Mt Anaka, are the masses of mankind who lack the individual or collective will to resist being propelled towards annihilation.

General Cummings is a sinister fascist, who has overweening personal ambition bolstered by great gifts for organization and by an imagination, which knows no restraint of human feelings. Cummings has distinct ideas about the direction of history. He firmly believes that the future belongs to the reactionary right and that the only morality of the future is a power morality. Power is the love of his life, and individual human beings are no more than chess pieces to be manipulated in his quest to satisfy his need. Therefore, taking advantage of a situation like war he exploits the men of his regiment and dispatches Croft's squad for a patrol of the Island, thereby risking many lives for a foolish enterprise. He desperately wants this mission to succeed because this would provide him with tremendous clout over his colleagues. Cummings' obsession with power dates from the First World War when he was a junior officer in the army and from the safety of his command bunker had watched an Allied attack upon the German lines and had been overwhelmed by an almost religious vision when he fired the weapon called the howitzer. As he watched his first battle unfold before his eyes he felt 'thrilled', was struck by the power of the commander, and thought, 'There were things one could do'. In another episode, the author once again reveals the General's euphoria over combat when Cummings contemplates the ramification of firing an artillery piece one night, realizing that handling of weapons during warfare gave him a feeling of tremendous power:

> "He dwelt pleasurably in many-webbed layers of complexity. The troops out in the jungle were disposed from the patterns in his mind, and yet at this moment he was living on many levels at once; in firing the gun he was a part of himself. All the roaring complex of odours and sounds and sights, multiplied and remultiplied by all the guns of the division, was contained in a few cells of his head, the faintest crease of his brain. All of it, all the violence, the dark coordination had sprung from his mind. In the night, at that moment, he felt such power that it was beyond joy; he was calm and sober." (*The Naked and the Dead,* 566-67)

The army as an institution moulds General Cummings and offers him an instrument for the implementation of his ideas. The General knows that in the army, all men should be arranged in ranks, on the fear ladder: "to make an army work you have to have every man in it fitted into the fear ladder" (*The Naked and the Dead,* 184) and that the army "functions best when you're frightened of the man above you, and contemptuous of your subordinates". Cummings believes that power must flow from top down and that each enlisted man must be broken in spirit so that he is ready to serve the machine of the 20th century technology. The General tells Hearn: "most men must be subservient to the machine, and it's not a business they instinctively enjoy" (*The Naked and the Dead,* 333). As a corollary, the menacing General looks upon men as mere 'fragments' of the war machine, cogs in the wheel and if one 'part' is destroyed it is simply replaced by another. This is in consonance with historian Erich Kahler's theory that during military training and while in combat soldiers who repeatedly and continuously handle weapons and other machinery related to warfare become like automatons (Kahler, 80). Technology according to Cummings is the greatest boon of the modern world and has great potential. However, the General does not want to look upon the beneficial aspects of technology but believes that it has the capacity to destroy the world within minutes. He is of the view that by manipulating technology he could become the most powerful individual on this Earth.

The love of sophisticated weapons, once again a product of mechanization and technological revolution is a great obsession with the General. In fact sometimes during his delusions he dreams that weapons are like human beings, having personalities of their own. Cummings mastery of men, of guns, and of concerted violence, gives him a feeling of power and satisfaction akin to the gratification of a sexual experience, but far more profound. The diabolical General informs Hearn that he desires Omnipotence. The Megalomaniac often has visions where he imagines himself as God, and the Island of Anopopei his Universe declaring 'If there is God, he's just like me.' His insatiable hunger for power makes him believe that after the war the army should take over the reins of the government and bring about order and discipline in the chaotic American society. One way of doing this would be to organize the civilian population of America in accordance with the 'fear ladder'.

The other character who represents fascism in the novel is Sergeant Croft. Croft is an illiterate army regular, and not an intellectual who like Cummings is committed to an ideology but is a symbol of fascism because of his love for violence. Croft is the instrument of Cummings theory, its practical application and is a primitive war lover who has become absolutely brutish during war. While the other soldiers of the I&R Platoon like

Stanley, Martinez, Brown and Ridges dread combat and are terrified when the bombardment of the Island begins, Croft longs for combat and unlike the other men is able to successfully repress his fear after the Japanese onslaught.

When he witnesses combat or handles weapons, mystical forces work within him as they do in the General and they touch the deepest and the most hidden recesses of his being. He is the most violent of Mailer's soldiers and no definite explanation is offered for Croft's nature, and no one knows why he is the way he is. It is clear, though, that he is completely self-centred. Mailer closes the Sergeant's 'Time Machine' portrait with an emphatic statement: 'I hate everything which is not in myself'. He is a perfectionist who disdains lesser men and has no friends in the platoon with the exception of Sergeant Martinez, the platoon's expert scout, whose competence he appreciates. Like General Cummings, Croft wants to become Omnipotent like God, but is unable to articulate his desire. However one episode that convinces him of his Omnipotence is when he predicts Hennessey's death and this actually happens as soon as the platoon arrives on the Island. After this episode Croft dreams about power and its tremendous potential but is unable to form a conscious plan towards the fulfillment of his ambition. His quest is instinctive and there is a crude vision about the achievement of his goal but there is nothing concrete on his mind. His morality, like the General's, is a 'power morality' and therefore, he is furious when Hearn is made the leader of the unit, which is sent on a patrol of the Island, and when Hearn dies his exhilaration at commanding the platoon is almost maniacal. For Cummings, power lies in technology and the ability to control men through fear. In Croft's case power lies in his ability to unleash violence upon other human beings whom he perceives as weaker than himself. He admires and embraces violence and enjoys killing and the soldiers fear him and hate him: "Listen, he's made of Iron. He's the one man I'd never cross. He's probably the best platoon sergeant in the army and the meanest. He just doesn't have any nerves" (*The Naked and the Dead,* 17).

Croft is not only a violent or sadistic man (although he reveals such characteristics in plenty) but also a man like the General whose sexual energies have been perverted. Cummings's homosexual tendencies are channelized into power manipulation but with Croft, the frustrated rage for sex is translated into hatred for everything outside himself. War has further aggravated these tendencies; for torturing and killing a Japanese prisoner and witnessing the death of one of his own men are experiences that raise him to a pitch of ecstasy. The knowledge of death is a source of power and a form of self-gratification for him. After Hearn's death, Croft becomes so intoxicated with a desire to be all-powerful that he even dreams of overwhelming Nature. As he has always looked upon Mt Anaka as a formidable enemy, he now wishes to overpower this adversary by making the men of his platoon climb its difficult terrain, using a situation like war to fulfill his personal ambition because deep down he realizes that the men who are under his control would obey him only during a conflict. Critics argue that the redoubtable mountain becomes the 'other', an object that resists his authority and is beyond his control and therefore *must* be moulded to serve his will. Croft wants to treat the mountain like the men of his platoon who fear him and obey him. His ascent of the mountain is purely for his own gratification, he has the power to compel the platoon to accompany him, and he uses it, even to the point of threatening to kill any soldier who resists. In fact, Private Roth has to give up his life in order to satisfy Croft's insane ambition.

However, despite his obsession with power and authority, Croft is also secretly afraid of his own bestiality, which has increased manifold during war and does not want to come face to face with his animal self. This realization dawns upon him as soon as the platoon begins its arduous journey on the mountain. Critics like Donald Pizer argue that the scaling of the mountain becomes for Croft "a journey into the primitive, animal, instinctive center of himself—a journey through a wild, unexplored, and difficult landscape to the pure and austere absolute center of his identity" (Pizer, 106). Croft undertakes this journey under the pressure of a compulsive desire, but he is also afraid, since its successful completion will result in the 'nakedness' of complete self-knowledge, the knowledge perhaps of his absolute bestial qualities. He grows increasingly anxious as he climbs because he senses that he has embarked upon an internal contest that will determine which pole of his nature would be successful. Mailer leaves it to the reader to decide what the contesting poles of Croft's temperament are: will or instinct? human or animal? Controller or controlled? However, Croft fails in scaling the mountain as the platoon runs into a hornet's nest. When the platoon finally returns to the beach to wait for their boat, the relief he feels deep within himself troubles Croft: "For that afternoon at least.... Croft was rested by the unadmitted knowledge that he had found a limit to his hunger" (*The Naked and the Dead,* 701). Further, on the landing craft as the platoon is returning to their bivouac, Croft comes to the realization that he needs the other men, that "he could not have gone without them. The empty hills would have eroded any man's courage" (*The Naked and the Dead,* 709). But despite this failure, Croft's hunger for power and control soon reasserts itself and his acknowledgement of his need for others is equally short-lived. As the men of the Reconnaissance platoon are being shipped out of Anoppopei to another Island. Croft dreams of another combat and is possessed by a strong desire to 'be in control of things'.

It is interesting and quite surprising that Croft is one character with whom Mailer too identified closely. Although when the novel was published the author criticized Croft for his terrifying appetite for violence and his love for killing, later in an interview with Paul Krassner reprinted in the *Presidential Papers* Mailer said that the character for whom he had secret admiration like Croft were violent people. Frederick Karl is of the opinion that Croft is Mailer's triumph and the author's attitude revolves not around Cummings or Hearn but Croft. Other critics like Richard Foster call Croft the real hero of the novel and believe that creating Croft's character came naturally to Mailer although Hearn and Cummings did create some problems. Foster believes that in Croft, one can see Mailer's 'hipster' of the future. He is the White Negro and a psychopath who smouldered with an endless hatred and personifies much that is essential to Mailer's philosophical psychopath. The author is fascinated by Croft and his personality. However, despite what Mailer says and what critics believe one cannot admire individuals like Croft because he has failed as a human being and is sans qualities like kindness, compassion and decency. His love for war evokes revulsion in the readers.

While Croft and Cummings stand on the side of fascism, Lieutenant Hearn is the liberal Marxist who opposes this philosophy. The Lieutenant is a man who opposes war and his worldview provides a positive point of resistance to the fascism of Cummings and Croft and to power in a generalized sense. Hearn belongs to a wealthy, upper class aristocratic family and is a graduate from Harvard who feels cast out and alienated from the American society. He does not like being an officer and does not want to feel superior to the enlisted soldier. He believes in egalitarianism and when Cummings tells him that during war fear works and in the army soldiers have to be dehumanized Hearn disagrees, saying that ultimately soldiers will rebel, as they will not continue being afraid for long. The Lieutenant believes that the war would produce a Marxist revolution and fascism would never triumph in America. A champion of equality, he resents the privileges he has enjoyed all his life, a rich father and a comfortable existence and feels disturbed about the fact that the soldiers live under terrible conditions, while the officers have plenty of comforts: "they slept with mud and insects and worms while the officers bitched because there were no paper napkins" (*The Naked and the Dead,* 79).

Mailer paints Hearn as an idealist who disdains others for not living up to his ideals. Hearn values his 'inviolate freedom' because he believes that it is what separates him from the herd of humanity and protects him from undergoing humiliation at the hands of officers in the army. For Hearn, freedom is a matter of personal integrity because he believes no one individual should be allowed to violate the integrity of another. Breach of integrity according to him is the 'ultimate issue' over which one could even fight with superior officers. Thus, after an episode during which the General forces him to pick up a cigarette butt, Hearn 'lay face down on his cot, burning with shame and self-disgust and an impossible impotent anger' (*The Naked and the Dead,* 336) because he considers the test of will with the General to have been 'an ultimate issue'. It had been a display of pure power on Cummings' part, meant to deliberately humiliate him, and he had failed to resist. Hearn feels that he has not stood up for his own values, for his belief in his own self-worth as an individual. The reader might interpret this as an overreaction on Hearn's part, as the issue is a trivial one but not for the Lieutenant because he believes that he has compromised with his honour and dignity.

Hearn makes attempts to resist Cummings' power morality and the tyranny of fascism but does not succeed. He resolves to give up his position as an officer and decides to become an enlisted soldier. But before he can take concrete steps in this direction he realizes that this would be a futile endeavour as it would neither win him friends from the cadre of officers nor any sympathy from the posse of enlisted men. Later, Hearn vows to resist fascism and imagines himself as an 'anti-fascist terrorist' but is never able to translate his dream into action because Mailer kills the idealistic Lieutenant through the machinations of Cummings' counterpart Croft.

However, critics point out that there are other reasons for Hearn's failure to challenge the tyranny of Cummings and Croft. During a conversation with the General about the war aims of America, Hearn is told by Cummings that 'deep down' the Lieutenant was in fact quite like himself. There is some truth in this statement, as Hearn's ideological beliefs appear quite confused. Although he is a liberal Marxist, he is sometimes forced to agree with Cummings' theories especially when he goes to the ship in order to bring back supplies for the men on the Island and has to bribe an officer on duty. Despite his egalitarianism the Lieutenant is deeply offended when a junior officer Kerrigan is rude to him. Regardless of his liberal inclinations Hearn admits that 'The General was having an effect on him' (*The Naked and the Dead,* 327) and perhaps secretly agrees that the army does function on a system of fear and a method of killing individuality and power flowing from top downward. The General considers Hearn's ideals to be misguided, if not downright insincere. He claims to be an egalitarian whose concern is that the enlisted men are treated fairly but when he realizes that the troops will hate him sooner or later despite what he does and that Croft is an effective leader because he is hated, he becomes depressed because the circumstances seem to prove the General's 'fear ladder' perspective on life. Yet, when Hearn actually has the opportunity to exercise power, to lead his platoon, he discovers that he enjoys it, and that this emotion was an extremely pleasurable one. When Hearn joins· the platoon there is an antipathy between him and the Sergeant and the officer realizes that he is a little afraid of Croft, just as he was afraid of General Cummings. But when Croft, Hearn's junior and an enlisted soldier (not an officer) tries to wrest the leadership of the platoon, Hearn resents his action deeply. Leadership was something that Hearn was beginning to enjoy and he realizes to his sudden amazement.

> "Leadership, it was as filthy as everything else, and he enjoyed it now...beyond Cummings was his own desire to lead the platoon...when he searched himself he was just another Croft." (*The Naked and the Dead,* 606)

Hearn too, has an element of Croft in him, that touch of evil, which perhaps all human beings have. However, when the platoon gets ambushed and Wilson is left behind wounded, Hearn is able to overpower the Croft in himself and decides to take the platoon back. When Hearn gets killed, Croft reassumes the charge of the squad.

The other character who represents a liberal philosophy is Red Valsen, who is also used by Mailer to articulate the viewpoint of the common soldier. Just as Croft is Cummings' enlisted counterpart, Red is Hearn's spiritual aide, the uneducated miner from Montana who believes in the innate goodness and decency of human beings. Red has been a wanderer since the age of eighteen, constantly fighting to maintain his identity in a world, which seeks to rob him of it. His wanderings have led him towards fatalism, which is a protective measure against the fear of death. Red is aware of the fact that during combat the long-range chances for survival are slim, but he responds in a very practical way and realizes there was nothing to do but to go from one day into the next. He is kind and considerate and possesses a deep feeling for his fellow soldiers but wants to keep these emotions under check because he 'always curdled before emotion' and is aware that a situation like war requires suppression of emotion. Initially like Hearn, Red too makes an attempt to counter the fascism of Croft but is unsuccessful. During a crucial incident as Croft forces the men of his platoon to scale Mt Anaka, Red opposes him and comes in direct confrontation with the Sergeant but when Croft threatens to shoot him he backs out, choosing life over death. However, Mailer demonstrates that Red is not the only one who is affected by the confrontation: "All of them felt a wretched embarrassment. Each man was trying to forget the way he had been tempted to shoot Croft and had failed" (*The Naked and the Dead,* 696). Power, or perhaps the will to use power, wins again, just as it did in the showdown between Cummings and Hearn. Mailer seems genuinely concerned about the effect that succumbing to power has on people, individually or *en masse.*

The other soldiers though they lack Red's insight, sympathy and integrity, are also aware of the abyss, which may swallow them at any moment. Brown, Stanley, Gallagher and Wilson are all types, the masses who cannot resist the forces of totalitarianism. All of them fear combat and suffer endlessly as they struggle through the dense, unfriendly forest and later while climbing Mount Anaka. Goldstein and Ridges display some individuality when they are suddenly brought to the forefront when Wilson is wounded and they are assigned to carry him back to the beach but they soon sink into the quagmire of anonymity like the rest of the soldiers. Mailer touches briefly upon another aspect of fascism that is anti-Semitism through the characters of Roth and Goldstein who are Jews. While Goldstein regards himself as a Jew, with a distinct Jewish identity, Roth sees himself as an American, with an American identity. However, Mailer does not take up the cause of the Jews in the novel and moves towards broader issues.

The conclusion of the novel is rather ambiguous as Mailer does not allow either fascism or liberalism clear victory in the novel. Some critics believe that the novel is written from the Cummings-Croft point of view because Croft was a character who fascinated Mailer and the author created Croft like characters in his subsequent works as well. In Mailer's prediction of the future, Croft is clearly the co-adjustor of ruthless reactionary assertion. However, the novel does not offer such a simplistic solution. It is true that Hearn is defeated, but both Croft and Cummings are defeated as well in their individual will to 'conquer', the world and destiny as they are undermined by the absurdities of chance. Croft and his platoon run in panic from a swarm of hornets and Cummings' plan to outflank the Toyaku line is thwarted by Dalleson's success, which too is achieved, by accident rather than design. In fact neither Croft nor Cummings is allowed a clear victory.

Critics like Nigel Leigh, Robert Solotaroff, and Richard Gilman are of the opinion that Mailer does not allow totalitarianism a victory in the novel because neither Cummings nor Croft represent totalitarianism completely as both these characters are intensely individualistic and hence cannot be the slaves of the machine, which represents totalitarianism. Jean Radford is of the view that in showing Cummings as a fascist, Mailer has domesticated this ideology 'mobilizing its appeal from a European to an American context'. Radford opines that Cummings' fascism is a peculiarly American brand combining individualism and idealism, with a dream of totalitarianism:

> "Cummings does not regard himself as a functionary of the military system, but rather stands outside its means. His ultimate goal is superhuman, to take charge of the Island, to subdue whatever lay between Hearn and himself and the 5000 troops against him, the terrain and circuits of chance he would mould. When Cummings is defeated, he wonders about his troops and about the fear ladder, which had ultimately, not been successful either for Cummings or Croft." (Radford, 145)

Leigh believes that similar is the case with Croft. Croft is outside any ideology or political categories. He is intensely individualistic, he is less racist, ethnocentric or anti-Semitic than most of the men under his command. He is the only character that one clearly remembers from among the GI's. None of the above critics under estimate the capacity for evil in Cummings or Croft. Leigh argues that while resisting the mechanistic efficiencies of the military as tending to degrade his own potentialities, Cummings nevertheless advocates a reductive standard for most of the rest of humanity, both he and Croft exemplify the iniquitous relationship between violence and power. Thus totalitarianism, despite Hearn's death and Red Valsen's shattering humiliation is not allowed a clear victory in the novel.

If the novel is not written from the point of view of Croft and Cummings, the point of view espoused by Mailer must be that of Hearn. But this does not seem to be the case either. Although Hearn is a radical liberal, as mentioned he does not so much represent liberalism, as the 'desire' to be liberal. Temperamentally, Hearn is an aristocrat, a counterforce to the values represented by Cummings or Croft. But Hearn's liberalism is a soft target, easily collapsing in the face of Cummings' theoretical rigours and proving no match for Croft's single mindedness. Hearn seems to be a man without stable convictions. As has been mentioned earlier, Hearn often feels like Croft and Cummings, but as their ideological opponent fails to convince as a character. He lacks those qualities that Mailer has always deemed admirable. When he looks at Mt Anaka all he can see is an image of defeat, while Croft is excited upon looking at the mountain and accepts the challenge of scaling it Leigh believes that Hearn does not show 'grace under pressure'. According to critics like Norman Page, "in Hearn one sees a feeble ideologue whose final decision is to retire from the struggle and to resign from the commission" (Page, 100).

The novel is written in a Marxist-Leninist vein and one wonders why Mailer does not allow radical liberalism to triumph in the novel. When Mailer was writing his novel, he was gradually becoming disillusioned with the Leftist Movement in America that had become very popular in the 1930s. During the decade following the war, the entire Left was in a crisis. Mailer wrote *The Naked and the Dead* while this dissolution of belief was going on around him, but he does not seem to have realized until he was in the middle of writing the novel that his liberal Leftist tradition had in the deepest sense failed him too. The disenchantment with the Left for those writers who had committed themselves began with the signing of the Nazi Soviet Pact of 1939. These intellectuals felt that the Russians had undercut Leftist idealism by participating in the pact. The belief in Communism started shaking with the beginning of the Cold War, especially in America as Mailer like other writers began to grow disillusioned with Communism. However, Diana Trilling argues that it was only Stalin's brand of Communism that Mailer abhorred; he continued to believe in the tenets of Marx and Trotsky. However, the process of disintegration was underway and Mailer's belief in the Leftist political ideology was being called into question. This perhaps explains the ambiguous ending of the novel where neither fascism nor liberalism is allowed a clear victory. Mailer seems to suggest that the future belongs not to Hearn or Croft or Cummings but to people like Dalleson who are the slaves of the system.

Mailer conceived his novel in Naturalistic terms. The author says of his technique "I didn't have much literary sophistication while writing *The Naked and the Dead*. I admired Dos Passos immensely and wanted to write a book. Critic Stanley Gutman sees evidence of determinism in all Mailer's later novels, but insists that only his first uses Naturalism to emphasize social determinism with a continuing accretion of detail which builds to a realization of the ponderous and pervasive power of circumstance in affecting human character and destiny" (Gutman, 15). In the novel, the individual is almost completely weighed down by the effects of his environment so much so, that individuals have little, if any, hope of overcoming past influences that have shaped them. Furthermore, Randall H. Waldron believes that the final pages of the novel leave the definite impression of man lost, helpless, and passive in the grip of the anonymity and meaninglessness of modern life. He sees the novel's central conflict as a struggle between the will to individual integrity and the depersonalizing, deterministic forces of contemporary life.

Much of the determinism, biological and sociological that is present in the novel is a part of Mailer's Naturalism. The antagonistic relationship between men and the natural world, a world Mailer consistently portrays as powerful, harsh, alien, and impenetrable, is invariably in the foreground in the novel. The play of pure chance in human life and the indifference of non-human nature that constitutes a barrier to human desires and purposes is a recurring motif in *The Naked and the Dead.*

Nature is indifferent to the designs of men who cannot overpower its force and nothing illustrates this point more dramatically than the failure of the patrol near the end of the novel to scale Mt Anaka despite the leadership of Croft, the most fanatically resolute character in the novel. The mountain fascinates Croft, he wants to overpower it but it is more powerful than him. Croft is closest to nature because he appears as a primitive, savage creature, but towards the end of the novel he fails to overwhelm it. Even Cummings feels a certain affinity with the natural world when he looks at Mt Anaka and indulging in a mystical mood, thinks that he and the mountain understood each other as both of them, were bleak and alone, commanding the heights. Yet, in reality this affinity is nothing more than a human conceit, for the readers are told that the mountain is a formidable enemy, and the terrible bombardment of the Island becomes insignificant before its might:

> "Mount Anaka rose out of a base of maroon coloured smoke. Implacably, despite the new purple robes at its feet, the mountain sat on the Island, and gazed out to the sea. The bombardment was insignificant before it." (*The Naked and the Dead,* 20)

The jungle too with its grass and plains appears as an agency of motiveless malignancy and in the initial phases of the campaign we are told 'the jungle was easily the General's worst opponent'. Furthermore, the General's efforts to tame nature by improving the headquarters' bivouac are all laid to waste in a matter of minutes by a sudden tropical storm. These storms break out frequently and while the men can kill the Japanese they find it difficult to weather the fiery tornados that lash the Island. Mailer gives a detailed description of one such storm in the novel. A soldier, Ridges, watching the hurricane realizes that man's existence is paltry before Nature's fury. The author describes how the jungle looks ominous as the sky becomes black and the deafening roar of the thunder threatens to shatter the firmament:

> "Ridges was watching the typhoon with panic and acceptance. The foliage of the jungle was churning turbulently, ... a vicious wind lashed at the tents. The rain came on softly, tapped against the rubber fabric of the shelter, and then began to drive harder. In only a few seconds it became furious with pellets like hail.... A few bursts of thunder sounded in the distance, and then a cloud shattered overhead." (*The Naked and the Dead,* 99, 101)

Even men like Cummings and Croft who strive for power, authority and Omnipotence fail to crush nature's strength. Mailer also discovers intransigence or an indifference that bespeaks the absence of any benevolent guiding power in the Cosmos. Man is conceived as a part of non-human Nature, neither better nor worse than any other part. Men can act like beasts as the drunken Americans demonstrate when they hunt for souvenirs among the dead Japanese. In this scene the stinking corruption of the flesh in death is brought home to us when Red Valsen quite unexpectedly perceives that: "their damn sure ain't anything special about a man if he can smell as bad as he does when he's dead" (*The Naked and the Dead,* 578). This decay puts man squarely in the world of Nature and by implication denies any part of him an escape into the world of spirit. In the general scheme of biological determinism men are nothing more than creatures subject to stimuli and response and are forced to recognize the ultimate helplessness of human will in directing human affairs. Critic Praful Kar expresses the view that in use of metaphors and overall vision bleakness, *The Naked and the Dead* is reminiscent of Hemingway's *A Farewell to Arms.* In the novel the author refers to the soldiers as ants who are being crushed by the powerful environment:

> "Mailer's treatment of soldiers as ants recalls Hemingway's parable of ants in *A Farewell to Arms*. In the parable, Frederick Henry, instead of becoming the Messiah of the ants, becomes their destroyer, and in his gratuitous act of killing Hemingway suggests the idea of randomness and indeterminacy in human existence, an idea, which stems from both Existentialism and Naturalism. In Mailer's novel actions have no causal relationships with each other; they happen without any logic or reason. His description of the army as a 'nest of ants wrestling and tugging at a handful of bread crumbs in a field of grass' suggests the ultimate vision of Nihilism and void." (Kar, 44)

The Naturalists were social critics as well and Mailer's social determinism seems to suggest that Man is caught in gigantic and vicious trap from which there is no escape. Kar argues that a sense of pessimism runs through the entire novel:

> "In it, human beings are treated as mere victims of accident and are devoid of any freedom of choice. The world seems to be dominated by the whims of three contending persons: General Cummings, Lieutenant Hearn and Sergeant Croft. The novel suggests a vision of pre-lapsarian paradise. In a Darwinistic war for survival there is neither victory nor defeat." (Kar, 44)

It is interesting to note that some critics, while acknowledging the Naturalism of the novel, have observed intimations of movement toward Existential ideas that are evident in Mailer's later novels. Foremost among these are Laura Adams, Raymond Wilson and Ihab Hassan who argue that in *The Naked and the Dead*, Mailer moves towards rudimentary Existentialism as in the novel's portrayal of war, 'absurdity prevails' and 'anxiety' is dramatized. These critics argue that in the novel characters, like Hearn, Valsen, Croft, Ridges, and Goldstein, are all seeking 'self-knowledge,' consciously or unconsciously. Kar is of the opinion that there is a curious blend of Naturalism and

Existentialism in the novel. Existentialism became popular in the United States in the 1950s, and in the wake of its popularity many writers tried to reflect the mood and temper of the movement. Kar believes that Existentialism got assimilated into Naturalism and became an integral part of American mainstream thought as in both movements, freedom was an elusive phenomenon and choice a difficult proposition.

Mailer debunks combat in *The Naked and the Dead* but also addresses larger issues. He raises questions like whether capitalism as a system will sustain America or will liberalism survive in a power hungry world. Mailer seems to suggest that America of the post 1945 period with its massive wealth, detailed organization and aggressiveness would slowly grind over poorer countries. He suggests that fascists were hungry for power but so are the Americans and appears to warn his readers about American 'Neo-Imperialism' that would prove detrimental to many countries in future.

Irwin Shaw: *The Young Lions* 4

The Second World War is the most comprehensively recorded war in American fiction. The war novelists covered all its aspects on all fronts including combat in the army, the navy and the air force. Some novelists focused on the activities of service and headquarter troops while others turned their attention to problems of command and the hunger for power displayed by influential military leaders. A persistent theme in many of the novels of the period is the moral degradation caused by war. Novelists like Hawkes, Vance Bourjaily, Robert Lowry and even Irwin Shaw uphold the idea that war leads to a total corruption of basic values like decency and compassion transforming human beings into virtual beasts and monsters, as they indulge in gruesome and merciless killing of their fellow human beings. The novels put forth the idea that during war Man can never completely conquer the enemy because the enemy is within himself, in his intellectual and appetitive failures. The wages of war are death and lead directly to the collapse of humanity and in a war torn world expiation of sins is not possible. Perhaps the most fearful and widespread component in this dreary fabric of disenchantment is the conviction that war and the army develop a sadistic killer instinct in men.

The issue of morality is especially important in Irwin Shaw's *The Young Lions*, published in 1948 and termed as a moral allegory by many critics. Morality is an important concern in all of Shaw's writing and he has been referred to as a "moral writer who conceives moral problems simply, feels them deeply and dramatizes them with often terrifying historical relevance" (Trilling, 325). Shaw's first novel *The Young Lions* is a story where good triumphs over evil and details the experience of three characters—Noah Ackerman, a Jewish American, Michael Whitacre, a dissolute Broadway actor and Christian Diestel, the evil Nazi soldier. In addition to the stories of these men Shaw graphically presents the European theatre of war and its major events like the Nazi occupation of Paris, the Allied invasion of France and the bombing of the city of London. Shaw also takes his readers to the deserts of North Africa where he has set a small portion of his novel against the backdrop of the Battle of El Alamein. In its devotion to historical panorama *The Young Lions* is different from the war novels of his contemporaries like Norman Mailer and James Jones. While *The Naked and the Dead* is set on a fictitious Island, *From Here to Eternity* is devoted to Jones's simultaneously brutal and nostalgic depiction of the old peacetime army that vanished after the Japanese bombing of Pearl Harbour, Shaw's ambition was to create a fictional overview of the war in Europe from three distinct perspectives and in addition Shaw also touches upon the theme of anti-Semitism in the novel.

The Young Lions was based on his personal experience in war as a warrant officer in the United States Army Signal Corps and he had served in Africa, France, England and Germany. After the war was over in 1945 he began working on his voluminous novel. However, war had been Shaw's subject even before he started writing *The Young Lions* and his play, *Bury the Dead* touches upon the theme of combat. Six soldiers in the second year of the war refuse to be buried, arguing that society has never given them an opportunity to fulfill their aims and ambitions in life. Despite desperate appeals from the members of their families and commands from their superior officers, the soldiers refuse to change their decision. At the end of the play, the warriors and their gravediggers walk off the stage, dramatizing their hatred of war. Leslie Fiedler writing about the play in *Commentary* said that the audience enthusiastically supported the soldiers as they walked portentously off the stage.

In many ways, *The Young Lions* is a typical war novel, based on the total plot device where the writer puts in every major event related to the war (quite like Herman Wouk's *War and Remembrance*) so that the novel becomes exceedingly capacious. However, Shaw's novel is extremely impressive as well because it questions why war was fought in the first place with the author raising a basic question in the novel—did decency alone win the war, and, if so, why is it not able to win peace? The novel presents the German side of the war, demonstrating through the characters of Christian Diestel and Lieutenant Hardenburg the terrible barbarity of Nazism. However, viewed in the larger perspective, it demonstrates the component of wickedness that grips every human being during warfare. The Allies claimed that the war was a battle of good versus evil. The Germans were brutal and bestial but so were the Allied forces. Although the author does not show us scenes of Allied barbarity in the novel, Shaw writes against combat with tremendous passion and punch and his picture of the war from the German side is utterly engrossing. Employing the technique of realism he reveals an eye for detail especially in his description of army life in the barracks and war scenes such as Rommel's retreat, which has been compared to Hemingway's description of the Caporetto retreat in *A Farewell to Arms*.

The action of the novel covers the period from New Year's Eve in 1938, until 1945 when Hitler's war machine was crushed by the Allied forces. The novel opens with a new and hopeful year but ironically the Second World War broke out in the same year that is 1939. Shaw begins the novel with the portrayal of a beautiful and serene Austrian village, simultaneously demonstrating the undercurrents of violence that threaten to shatter the peace of not only the pastoral surroundings of the village but also the world. This happens when an American lady Margaret Freemantle is molested by an Austrian named Frederick and when she manages to escape from his clutches she meets Christian Diestel who praises Hitler's Anschluss (the violent and forcible union between Austria and Germany) and also upholds the dictator's views on Jews as being correct and just.

The novel delineates experiences of three young men who get involved in the conflagration. The drama of their lives, their joys and sorrows, acts of cowardice and instances of bravery are played out against the backdrop of World War II. The first of these men is Noah Ackerman an American Jew, the introvert son of a Polish immigrant who came to America in 1918. Noah regards himself as an American and does not give importance to his Jewish identity, but his war with anti-Semitism begins soon after his father's death and turns into a full-fledged battle when he joins the prejudiced American army that humiliates him for being a 'Jew boy'. Thus along with fighting the external enemy he also has to fight the 'enemy within'. Before joining the army Noah marries Hope, a girl from Vermont who becomes his source of strength as he battles his opinionated comrades in the army.

Michael Whitacre is the profligate Broadway stage manager and Hollywood theatre actor. A debauched lifestyle and a disintegrating marriage are distinguishing features of his life when he is introduced to the reader. When Michael makes an appearance in the novel he is contemplating about the 'unreality' of his existence and making an attempt to find 'meaning' in his muddled life. Ultimately his disillusionment with the theatre in Hollywood and New York makes him join the army, which becomes a means of escaping his sordid situation. However, the pointlessness of his existence continues to haunt Michael even as he participates in the action of the war against Germany. The actor finally finds a purpose in his life when he joins Noah in his war against anti-Semitism and vows to remain a protector of the 'underdogs' all through his life.

Christian Diestel is the Austrian ski instructor who joins the Nazi party because he admires Hitler and supports his violent policies especially his extermination of Jews. Although he is an Austrian, unlike the people of his country he supports the Anschluss and joins the Nazi party becoming a true Nazi soldier, pitiless and barbarous. Shaw reveals Diestel's disintegration from a human being to an animal as he endlessly tortures, kills and indulges in violence. Finally, as the war draws to a close, the three men confront each other outside a concentration camp located in Germany's Black Forest. There, Michael finds the true meaning of his aimless life when he kills the villain Diestel who has murdered the innocent Noah. There are a few minor characters in the novel who play important roles. Lieutenant Hardenburg is Christian's mentor and he becomes a symbol of evil in the novel. Hardenburg's wife Gretchen, a promiscuous woman comes to represent the changing morality of a war torn world.

The Young Lions is voluminous in scope and critics have called it structureless and formless because the stories of the three characters do not have a link. John Aldridge in his book *After the Lost Generation* expresses the opinion that the novel has structural complexities. Although Shaw does try to connect the experiences of the major characters through the minor characters who serve as links connecting Diestel, Whitacre and Ackerman, the parallel experiences do not "grow organically out of the novel's meaning", and are "a system of carefully contained parallels, near parallels and pseudo parallels which give only the appearance of unity" (Giles, 82). However, some critics are of the opinion that the character that can be called a 'linking character' in the novel is Margaret Freemantle, who is the first character to be introduced. Margaret is a beautiful young girl who is in the Austrian village when the novel opens in 1938 and is almost raped after a New Year's Eve party. After the party while Margaret is asleep in her hotel room a young man named Frederick (the son of the owners of the hotel where Margaret is staying) enters her room and makes an attempt to molest her. The girl resists Frederick's coercion and manages to escape from the hotel. After her escape she meets Diestel and both argue about the evils of Nazism. The next morning, Margaret leaves with her lover, a Jewish doctor named Joseph. She reappears later in the novel at a party given by Whitacre in Pennsylvania with the radio carrying the news of the Nazi occupation of Paris. Subsequently, she and Michael have a meaningful relationship.

Despite the fact that Margaret appears infrequently in the novel she carries much of the novel's 'structural load'. Shaw first uses her conversation with Diestel to expose the inner corruption of the ski instructor who despite sympathizing with her after her molestation appears to be a fundamentalist supporting Nazism and all its evils. Her relationship with her lover Joseph, the European Jew threatened by the Holocaust, foreshadows the introduction of Noah Ackerman the American Jew who is killed in Europe. Critic James Giles believes that Margaret has a considerable role to play in the novel and she is a sympathetic character who represents innocence and is a champion of peace. She is horrified when Diestel supports the massacre of Jews and is horrified that he admires a dictator like Hitler. Her goodness is contrasted with Diestel's monstrosity and she also acts as a moral guide to Whitacre.

Although Margaret is meant as a largely sympathetic character she also represents an American innocence, which Shaw finds dangerous because it is a result of superficiality of intellect. At the party given by Whitacre she is outraged at any suggestion of America entering the war even as the radio carries the news of Nazi occupation of Paris. Michael tells her that 'you are living in the wrong year' (*TYL*, 150). Thus, despite being a decent and good human being Shaw reveals that her limitations of intellect and perception are severe. She represents the decent American, well intentioned but dangerous because of her refusal or inability to comprehend reality. However, Shaw does not develop Margaret's character and she soon disappears from the novel.

Initially, the author had an extremely elaborate idea for *The Young Lions* and had decided to link the stories of Whitacre, Diestel and Ackerman with a 'fourth Character', the bullet fired by Whitacre that kills Diestel in Black Forest. Shaw said in an interview:

> "I wanted to show it as lead in the ground, the miners that got it out, the engineers, the smelters, the sorters, the packagers, then the long chain of supply in the army that put the bullet finally in Whitacre's cartridge belt. My idea was to show that we are all linked in this world—the most sophisticated, the most primitive—the link being, in our time, death. There are other links, of course, but the strongest and most fundamental one in our century is death." (Giles, 79-80)

The central thematic concern of *The Young Lions* is the moral and ethical choices made by human beings during a situation like war. Some individuals despite witnessing the suffering, trauma and violence of war choose the path of righteousness while others deliberately and wilfully embrace wickedness. Noah and Michael begin their journey through the course of the novel with an avoidance of moral commitment and end it with devotion to principle. On the other hand, Christian begins with an abstract but a monstrous set of ethical values and consistently acts upon them until by the end of the novel he has become absolutely depraved. However, Diestel dies at the hands of Michael. The novel thus can be interpreted as an allegory where good triumphs over evil and the benevolent Whitacre obliterates the malevolent Diestel. Certain characters in the novel like Margaret, Noah's wife Hope and Christian's superior officer Lieutenant Hardenburg too have allegorical functions to perform.

In *The Young Lions* Christian Diestel's transformation is the most significant and his conversion progresses from latent to active monstrosity in the novel. He is introduced to the reader in the first chapter as a: "Tall, slender young man, with a solemn abstracted face and close cut black hair, his skin burned dark by the sun, his eyes light and almost golden with yellow flecks you find in an animal's eyes" (*TYL*, 6).

At the outset itself Shaw uses animal imagery to describe Diestel's personality. This imagery continues throughout the novel as in successive chapters Shaw uses terms like 'feral' 'beast', 'monster', 'brute' and 'wild' to describe Christian and in the last chapter when Christian has become an absolute fiend and is stalking Noah, his prey in the Black Forest, Shaw uses words like 'crouching' and 'circling' to reiterate the animal image.

In the first chapter it is easy to discern that he does not have a very strong code of ethics. After Margaret escapes from Frederick, she meets Christian. Despite the fact that he condemns Frederick there are hints of his own desire for a sexual encounter with Margaret, something that she does not understand. More than his sexual hypocrisy however, is the moral values that Christian proclaims to Margaret which reveal his capacity for barbarity. First drawing her attention towards Austria's poverty he supports the forcible union of Austria and

Germany and states that the amalgamation of the two countries would be beneficial for the Austrian economy. Further, he dismisses any form of socialism as absurd. What is most disturbing about his conversation with Margaret is the fact that he supports the extermination of the Jews justifying it on the grounds that:

> "If the only way you can get a decent and ordered Europe is by wiping out the Jews, then we must do it. A little injustice for a large justice...the end justifies the means." (*TYL,* 18-19)

An individual who possesses the ability to minimize genocide as a 'little injustice' definitely has the potential for unlimited monstrosity. Through Christian, Shaw shows the main tenets of the Nazi philosophy, which was in fact a perversion of the viewpoint of Friedrich Nietzsche.

A crucial first step in Christian's movement from covert to overt monstrosity occurs when his jeep is ambushed by some members of the French underground outside Paris. During the ambush scene, Christian kills his first Frenchman and does not 'feel anything special'. He is praised by his superior Hardenburg for doing this and as the novel progresses he comes to emulate Hardenburg more and more and becomes a virtual reincarnation of this evil man. The scene has certain allegorical elements because of the presence of an allegorical figure in the episode. A young German soldier named Kraus is killed in the ambush immediately after bragging that he will kill a Frenchman in order to avenge his father who had lost a leg in the First World War. Kraus is a staunch disciple of an officer Sergeant Himmler, a mediocre who is supposedly an allegorical representation of Heinrich Himmler, an important member of Hitler's SS. It was believed that Heinrich Himmler was an average individual who rose to power and prominence in the Nazi Party through dishonourable means. It was this man who at Hitler's behest sent thousands of Jews to the gas chambers and even exhorted young men to join the German army and aid in wiping out the enemies of the Third Reich. Shaw reveals that the naïve, innocent Kraus intent on killing embodies Germany's potential to be led into unprecedented areas of sub-human actions by monsters like Heinrich Himmler, the mass murderer.

Diestel's further moves from covert to overt monstrosity during the North African campaign, which is being led by Lieutenant Hardenburg. As Christian's unit is proceeding through the African desert, they ambush a group of British soldiers. Hardenburg hums as he waits to give a signal to open fire on the soldiers: "Hardenburg didn't stir. Still the smile, still the tuneless humming...the sound was foolishly loud and metallic. He's enjoying it Christian thought, looking back once more to Hardenburg" (*TYL*, 202).

Although Diestel is outraged by the Lieutenant's humming, later, in a parallel scene, he hums to himself before giving orders to open fire on American troops. The phrase 'he didn't feel anything special' recurs throughout the novel and is associated with Diestel's endless cruelty. For instance, after rounding up some French resistance members for the SS and hearing their screams as they are being tortured, Diestel realizes that 'it hadn't been so bad' and 'he didn't feel anything special'. The second stage in his degeneration from latent to active monstrosity takes place when he commits himself to Hardenburg's discipleship, once again intentionally and persistently choosing evil over good. He falsely identifies two Frenchmen as the murderers of a soldier named Behr and watches their execution after the SS has tortured them. He also betrays his one time friend the photographer Brandt to the SS as a traitor and does it significantly in the name of Hardenburg: "Better friends than Brandt had died beside him for four years; should Brandt be left alive to suck on Hardenburg's bones?" (*TYL*, 578-79). Brandt the photographer represents art and for that reason a muted albeit tacit opposition to Nazism and Diestel the true disciple of this philosophy cannot tolerate this antagonism.

Towards the end of the novel Christian becomes an animal devoid of any traces of humanity. The year is 1945 and the German army is in complete disarray; he is involved in his own retreat and personal survival is his only goal. By this time Diestel is contemptuous of the Nazis because he believes that Germany lost the war by refusing to be harsh and brutal enough. The soldier stumbles into a Nazi concentration camp located near the Black Forest and instead of repugnance and moral pain at the sight of gas chambers and skeletal figures in prison uniforms he is outraged by the smell of the camp and the 'incompetence of the camp commanders'. By now, he is an absolute fiend. Charles Rolo expresses the view that it is allegorically sound for this final stage of his metamorphosis to take place in a setting symbolic of twentieth century's most infamous capitulation to brutality. The critic is of course referring to the Holocaust and its impact on the Jewish people of Europe. After the American troops arrive at the concentration camp, Christian hides in the forest in order to save his life.

The allegorical role-played by Hardenburg and his wife is crucial to Diestel's transformation. The Lieutenant and his wife Gretchen become symbols of Diestel's inner monstrosity. In a crucial and one of the most violent scenes in the novel as Diestel and the Lieutenant are escaping after the German defeat in the North African campaign, a mortar shell hits their motorcycle, and Hardenburg is seriously injured and his face is mutilated. In the hospital, the Lieutenant attempts to maintain an illusion of confidence by telling Diestel that the doctors have promised him a new face and that his wound will help his post-war career in politics. In these scenes Hardenburg appears as a megalomaniac who declares that Germany must always be kept in a state of war and lectures Christian on the future of Nazism and the war aims of Germany stating that in order to win the war the country needed to resort to extreme aggression and violence without feeling guilty or remorseful:

> "If we announced to the world that for every day of war, we would kill one hundred thousand Europeans, and kept to our promise, how long do you think the war would last? We should print lists of names with photographs.... We are suffering because our conduct is not yet as mature as our philosophy...when we overcome remorse we shall be the greatest people in Western history.... Killing is an objective act and death is a state beyond right and wrong. I can kill a nineteen-year-old lieutenant two months out of Oxford and

> leave three dozen Germans to die on a hill with exactly the same calculation, because I know these things." (*TYL,* 291-92)

He regards war, as the most 'fascinating' of all pursuits because in his opinion it fits the ultimate nature of Man, which is predatory and egotistic, and is also of the view that a soldier must never want peace. He tells Christian that the mutilation of his face 'does not disturb him too much' and that he is aware that when the bandages are taken off the sight would be horrifying, but being a soldier the Lieutenant would be able to suppress his fright and revulsion successfully.

The Lieutenant appears as a madman and his philosophy (although exaggerated) closely resembles the views expressed by Hitler in his autobiography *Mein Kampf.* As Christian leaves the hospital and returns to combat he absorbs his mentor's obsessive love for killing. Hardenburg has his face blown away metaphorically exposing inner monstrosity. Symbolically, Diestel has become more than his Lieutenant's disciple, he is the monster resurrected and magnified.

The other allegorical character is Hardenburg's wife Gretchen who is a symbol of moral corruption. While Christian comes to Berlin on leave he meets Hardenburg's wife and seduces her. Gretchen on her part introduces him to deviate sexual experiences, which are new and somewhat shocking to Christian. The Lieutenant's wife works for the Nazi Propaganda Ministry and is a favourite sexual partner of high-level party members. In one crucial passage, Shaw describes the material possessions which she has collected from her influential lovers: "A student of economics could have pieced together the story of German conquest in Europe and Africa merely from the stores tucked carelessly away in Gretchen's apartment" (*TYL,* 163). Christian realizes that she is above ordinary morality, beyond it. Giles is of the view that Gretchen is the 'symbolic prostitute of Nazism'. He further expresses the view that:

> "The description of her closet, full of material possessions, recalls the passage in *Tender is the Night* in which Fitzgerald denounces the excesses of American

> capitalism by describing the world's economy as functioning as only for the pleasure of Nicole Diver. Compared to Gretchen, however, Nicole is angelic just as Nazism represents an evil considerably in excess of laissez faire American capitalism." (Giles, 85)

It is significant to note however that Christian does have fleeting moments of goodness and decency when he sees a vision of Margaret Freemantle twice in the novel. Margaret represents good values and humanity, but Diestel is successfully able to brush away these visions and subdue the human being in him. In another episode in the novel set against the backdrop of Normandy Landings, Christian and the members of his unit are stranded on a beach and are struggling to survive as the German army is in total disarray. At this juncture Christian is accosted by a soldier named Behr who tells him that the war is over and the Germans have been defeated: "The animal is slowly being driven into his last corner; the human being is preparing his final punishment" (*TYL,* 432). Behr then suggests that if the German's wished to save themselves they must rebel against Hitler and negotiate peace with the Allies. Diestel seems to listen seriously to Behr and even has a momentary vision of Margaret Freemantle, but before he can commit himself either way an Allied plane strafes the beach, Behr is seriously wounded and Christian rushes to get medical help. Behr's plan is based on the actual attempt by certain high-ranking members of the German army to assassinate Hitler towards the end of the war. The scene suggests that Christian is momentarily tempted by the idea of overthrowing Hitler (the symbol of evil) and for a fleeting moment makes an attempt to select good over evil. However, when Christian returns Behr is dead and once again suppressing decency and humanity he knowingly chooses evil and while escaping from the combat zone snatches the bicycle of a young boy, murders him and rides away to safety.

Critics like William Stratt and Aldridge however, argue that Diestel's characterization, as a total monster is difficult to believe. Aldridge even goes so far as to call him a bravely dedicated but ultimately defeated German soldier who is gradually brutalized by the war. On the other hand, Peter G.

Jones avers that: "Christian is a good man who dies in the service of a cause unworthy of him. His weakness is that his concepts of order and nationalism mean more to him than human lives" (Jones, 90). Despite what these critics say, Christian operates from a corrupt ethical basis and hence can only degenerate. His name carries considerable irony as he totally lacks in the Christian virtues of piety, goodness and compassion. He is the true Nazi, the atheist who does not show respect towards religion. Moreover, it is not difficult to believe that men like Christian existed in Nazi Germany. During the Nuremberg trials, the atrocities committed by Nazi soldiers were revealed to the world and many of these individuals were like Diestel.

Noah Ackerman is an antithesis to Christian who is introduced to us as an individual who is trying to deny the need for an ethical code, but is forced by circumstances and his own innate decency to formulate one. The acceptance of and pride in his Jewish heritage become the central concern in Noah's code. Like Diestel, Noah is also compelled to make a choice and he has to choose between a denial of his ethnic identity and its recognition and ultimately he accepts the latter. Some critics therefore have interpreted the novel as a dramatic affirmation of faith in the struggle of the Jew for equality in the modern world. Through Noah's character Shaw not only wants to remind his readers about the heinous crimes committed during the war by the Nazis against the European Jews, but also wishes to draw their attention to the fact that animosity towards this community existed in a democratic country like America as well. As a child of Jewish immigrants from Russia Shaw too may have faced the kind of prejudice that is faced by Ackerman in the American army.

Noah is introduced to us on the deathbed of his father as a shy introvert, who does not have very strong opinions on any subject and does not wish to see himself as a Jew, but rather looks upon himself as an American. His dying father Jacob is dictating a letter to his brother Israel (Noah's uncle) in Hamburg Germany and in a state of delirium tells his son that 'they are burning my brother Israel in a furnace'. The symbolism is more than evident here. The name Israel is a symbol of the Jews and the 'burning' refers to the Holocaust which had begun in Europe in 1938. Noah is repulsed by the lies that the old man is sending to his brother, giving a false account of his material prosperity and social prominence, claiming to have seven children when in fact Noah is his only child. However, a few seconds before his death Jacob abruptly reverses his lies and states the truth about his life in America:

> "I have led a miserable life and I have cheated everyone and I drove my wife to her death and I have only one son and I have no hope for him." (*TYL*, 49)

After his father's death Noah does not wish to be identified by his Jewish legacy and his initial response at Jacob's death is relief at being freed from the weight of his heritage. Leaving the dead man in the house Noah goes out to arrange for his cremation, immediately encountering anti-Semitism when an undertaker refuses to perform the funeral of his father and his wife declares: "He don't burn Kikes. Happy New Year" (*TYL*, 53). These words recall Jacob's words about the burning of Israel in Europe. A miserable Noah then spends the night with a prostitute and cremates his father the next morning with the help of a Jewish undertaker.

Subsequently he falls in love with Hope Plowman and once again encounters prejudice when he goes to meet her family in Vermont. As Noah and Hope's father go for a walk in the country, the latter informs Noah about his family's New England Yankee heritage and admits that he would have preferred his daughter to marry someone with similar, defined roots. Noah, whose own father was a personification of the homeless wandering Jew, listens in despair as Mr. Plowman expresses his ignorance and suspicion of Jewish people. However, Hope's father abruptly declares that since his daughter and Noah are so insistent about their marriage he would be unable to change his daughter's decision and with resignation accepts Noah as his son-in-law.

Ackerman's full-fledged war with anti-Semitism begins when he enlists in the army after the attack on Pearl Harbour. His enlistment has nothing to do with Jewish pride because he joins the army as an American who is out to fight the Germans. He is however, forced to change his opinion after he goes for training down South, where he becomes a target of harassment by two anti-Semitic officers Captain Colclough and Sergeant Rickett. The totalitarian set up of the army shows great hostility towards Ackerman who is forced, much against his wishes, to forge a Jewish identity for himself. Colclough seizes three books from Noah, Joyce's *Ulysses*, which he calls a 'filthy dirty book' *The Collected Poems of T.S. Eliot*, and a collection of George Bernard Shaw's dramatic essays. Colclough thus represents the totalitarian regime, which attempts to destroy Noah's sensitive and intellectual temperament. Thereafter, the two officers systematically inflame the rest of the company into a physical and mental torture of the Jew.

Ackerman's transformation from an introverted, timid human being begins when ten soldiers of the company harass him by stealing ten dollars from his wallet and making him a butt of anti-Jewish jokes. A punitive Noah insists on fighting all the ten men in his company, asking Whitacre (who has been drafted into the same unit) to be his second. He is brutally beaten each time, but the superior officers of the army do nothing to stop the fight. After the eighth fight, a soldier named Fein, the only other Jew in the Company, visits Noah. Fein is physically strong and therefore safe from the kind of brutality Noah is receiving but he urges him to accept Anti-Semitism as a reality passively without fighting back. However, events and circumstances have compelled Ackerman to have very strong opinions about his Jewish identity: "I want every Jew...to be treated as though he weighed two hundred pounds" (*TYL*, 330).

Finally he beats the ninth man named Brailsford soundly but nobody congratulates him on his victory. Disgusted by the acrimony of his prejudiced colleagues Noah deserts the army. His crusade had been to win however painfully the respect of other men and the fact that he could not was revealed by their refusal to acknowledge his triumph. Immediately after his desertion, however, Noah is filled with remorse and gives himself up to the army establishment in New York. He is imprisoned and admits before the authorities that his action was grievously wrong. When a pregnant Hope visits Noah at the army prison, a bureaucrat named Lewis explains to her that due to the 'extenuating circumstances' of his desertion the army will not press charges against him but Noah must return to his old Company. When he learns of Hope's pregnancy, Ackerman realizes that he has new responsibilities and agrees to return to his old outfit. However, this time when he returns he is a changed person. His war with the system makes him carry a knife, which he threatens to use at any sign of intimidation. The men of his Company appear different too, as they greet him with the news that after his desertion three other men followed suit, resulting in Colclough's upbraiding by his superior officers. In addition they give him a package of the three books that had been appropriated by Colclough. Noah realizes that finally his truce with the army had been made:

> "He realized that his personal armistice with the Army had been made. It had been made on lunatic terms, on the threat of the knife and the absurd prestige of his opposition to authority, but it was real...." (*TYL*, 353-54)

However, this is only a partial victory. Although a humane officer Captain Green replaces the diabolical Sergeant Colclough Noah soon learns that men like Sergeant Rickett are still an integral part of this totalitarian institution. During the Normandy Landings, Noah courageously saves two men of his Company from the German bombardment and escapes from the enemy lines, even drawing a map of crucial enemy positions at the back of Hope's and his baby's photograph. Upon his return to the Company, Green lauds him for his brave action and promises him a medal but Rickett taunts him with an offensive remark: "Oh Christ, we still got the Jew" (*TYL*, 509). Noah's reaction to Rickett's insult constitutes the last phase of his personal armistice with the army. He now realizes that his enemy is the cumulative anti-Semitism of the Company's enlisted men and perhaps his entire country. Thus, Rickett has absolved him from ever trying to prove anything again. His main aim would now be to survive the war and return to his wife and child and his plans for the future too are clearly laid out—After the war, Noah and a man named Johnny Burneckner (who has become his staunch friend and ally after the dramatic escape from the enemy lines) will work together in Iowa. Burnecker's uncle owns a newspaper in this small town and has promised to hire Noah as a reporter. The duo decides that Noah, Hope and the baby would live quietly and happily in this small American town close to Burnecker. As he plans his future, Noah comes to regard Iowa as a city that would be a refuge from the onslaught of anti-Semitism. However, life with its strange twists and turns had other plans for both of them. While Burnecker dies of tuberculosis of the brain, Christian Diestel brutally murders Noah in the Bavarian forests of Germany, thereby symbolically killing righteousness and morality.

It is significant to note that his traumatic experiences in the army do not transform Noah into a bitter and cynical individual as he continues to thrive on the hope that good will triumph over evil in a world plagued by wickedness, malevolence and inequity. Noah dies with a burning optimism that justice will finally prevail on earth. Noah chooses hope over despair and this therefore becomes a very important word in his life. To begin with his wife's name is Hope and she embodies the hope of self-transcendence for Noah. Further, as he fights the ten men of his Company it is hope that leads him towards victory. Noah dies after having chosen and accepted his Jewish identity. His last words to Michael are that just and humanitarian people like Lieutenant Green would ultimately run the world:

> "The human beings are going to be running the world! There's a lot of Captain Greens! He's not extraordinary! There're millions of them!" (*TYL*, 680)

Critics have called Michael Whitacre's characterization as the weakest part of the novel with James Giles expressing the view that Shaw was writing about a type he knew when he created the New Yorker, but the character rarely rises above the level of a type. Although he is one of the three protagonists of the novel Shaw does not subject him to an in-depth analysis. When Michael makes an appearance like Noah he is sans an ethical code, in fact he has no purpose and often feels 'unreal', disillusioned and restless. Like other characters, the Broadway theatre actor too is compelled to make an ethical choice towards the end of the novel. After avenging Noah's death he chalks out a mission for himself and that is that he would fight for the rights of all the oppressed and exploited people of the world. Thus Michael gives himself a purpose in life. In the beginning of the novel Shaw reveals him as a 'playboy' but despite this image he is basically a decent human being, an intellectual and to a certain extent an idealist even though he is a part of the degenerate Hollywood world. However, a negative facet of Michael's temperament is his selfishness and indecisiveness.

He is introduced to the reader at a New York party where a man named Parrish (who has returned from the Spanish Civil War), shames him into donating money for the Loyalist cause. Later, at the same party, Parrish saves a drunken playwright (Michael's friend) from suicide while Michael, helpless to act, stands by. Parrish who has courage to fight for the cause in Spain is a living reproach to Michael who is just wasting his life. Donating money towards the Loyalist cause is a desperate attempt to hide his weakness and cowardice. After the suicide episode, Michael realizes the horrible meaninglessness of his existence as he comes to the conclusion that there was no form and honour in his life, and everything disappeared in a blur of alcohol, indecency, infidelity, and indecision. In Michael's case, honour and form is difficult to attain because he has to overcome his own weakness of character, which resorts to cynicism in the face of difficult and complex problems. The first crucial moment in Michael's struggle for meaning is a chance meeting with Margaret Freemantle, which results in a two-year long relationship. This relationship is quite different from the ones he has had earlier as he honestly loves Margaret and, as a result, begins to come to grips with his own habitual weakness.

As America is dragged into the war after Pearl Harbour, Michael does not initially enlist in the army, as he is terribly afraid. However, gradually he overcomes his fear as he watches men younger than himself voluntarily getting themselves drafted and being shipped out to European and the Pacific fronts. Overcome by a sense of shame he decides to enlist and finally joins the infantry instead of the Special Services that his

Broadway connections could easily have obtained for him. He is drafted into the same company as Noah and takes another step towards finding a purpose in his life when he serves as Noah's second while training in Florida. Michael is horrified by the kind of treatment being meted out to Ackerman, which is a gross violation of basic human rights. After this episode he decides to become an officer so that he would be in a position to protect all the underdogs of the army. However, his request is denied when the FBI discovers that he had donated money for the Loyalist cause in Spain. The irony here is more than apparent, Whitacre had donated money to salvage his conscience but this results in the destruction of his genuine desire for a purpose in life. A disgusted Michael shocked and revolted by the unjust treatment meted out to him refuses to fight back and requests a transfer out of the infantry. Once again Shaw highlights another weakness in his character, the inability to fight against injustice in a dogged and persistent manner. In this respect Michael is a sharp contrast to Noah who fights unfairness despite being at a disadvantage *vis-à-vis* the other men of the Company. Michael then becomes a Civil Affairs officer, feeling guilty about his non-combatant status, continuing to feel dissatisfied with his life but resisting the impulse to ask for a transfer back to the infantry despite the worry that:

> "A man...should have been able to emerge with a key, a key to wars and oppression, a key to unlock the meaning of Europe and America." (*TYL*, 587)

In a scene, which is reminiscent of his inability to save the drunken playwright from suicide, Michael finds himself momentarily trapped in German ambush in an occupied French village, but cannot act to protect the villagers or even himself. When members of his unit arrest two badly injured German soldiers Michael cannot bring himself to murder them, as they are merely boys in their teens, even as the enraged villagers pressurize him to kill the enemy. A woman, Mrs. Dumoulin tells him that the French who have been living under the German autonomy for the last four years cannot display any compassion towards the 'barbarians'. Michael is torn between a desire to murder the boys and to protect them from the wrath of the people and while he is debating upon a course of action his colleague Keane picks up his rifle and shoots the two soldiers. Although the former Broadway actor despises Keane for doing this he also realizes that he has been a miserable failure as a soldier. While Michael had faltered and fumbled, Keane had behaved like a true soldier and without fear and hesitation obliterated the enemy.

Ironically, later in the novel Michael is awarded the 'Purple Heart' not for any act of bravery but through sheer coincidence. Following the Allied occupation of Paris, Michael is celebrating with another officer when they are run over by a taxicab. He suffers a broken leg and as he is recuperating at the hospital in the same ward as those injured during combat, an officer of the army while on a visit to the hospital awards all the wounded soldiers the Purple Heart without even asking Michael the cause of his injury. Consumed with remorse, Michael now insists that he be transferred back to the infantry near a combat zone. Acceding his request, the army transfers him back to his old outfit. The irony of Michael's receiving a Purple Heart for being run over by a Parisian taxicab symbolizes the fact that Michael would never have been able to act on his own had external events not interceded.

Michael is thereafter reunited with Noah Ackerman, who helps in the attempt to give meaning to his life and contributes towards his ethical development. In killing the unethical monster Diestel, Michael is finally able to triumph over the weak side of his nature. The novel's closing hope rests with Michael. The Hollywood playboy, who could not save a friend from suicide, but tracks down Noah's murderer and kills him. The novel's hope is that Michael would be one of the 'human beings' who will run this world. The Nazi soldier's death also reveals that good ultimately triumphs over evil. It is, however, unfortunate that Shaw does not develop Michael's character expansively and he appears what William Stratt refers to as an animated cardboard prop, who, caught midway between idealism and opportunism, flounders recklessly drifting with the inertia of war.

Irwin Shaw uses a realistic technique in *The Young Lions* and the novel is set against the backdrop of real historical events with most of the action taking place against the background of historical battles. The novel opens in the year 1939, after the forcible union of Austria and Germany, which was known as Anschluss. In 1938, Austrian chancellor Kurt Schuschnigg, in a last bid to retain Austrian independence, announced a referendum to determine independence or union with Germany. Germany then pressurized Schuschnigg into handing over power to the Nazi party and when the German troops entered into Austria to enforce the Anschluss, no fighting ever took place. The international response to the Anschluss was mild, the Allies only lodged diplomatic protests, and no concrete action was taken to reverse the Anschluss, even though the Allies were, on paper, committed to upholding the terms of the Treaty of Versailles, which specifically prohibited the union of Austria and Germany. The opening chapter of the novel sets its moral tone by demonstrating that Hitler's action was morally reprehensible.

Yet another historical event which is given great importance in the novel is the Battle of France. This Battle refers to the German invasion of France and the Low Countries, which resulted in the outflanking of the Maginot Line, a front created by the French for their protection. Paris was occupied by the Germans and the French government fled to Bordeaux. France capitulated to Germany after the French Second Army Group was forced to surrender. *The Young Lions* describes the Occupation of Paris in detail. The victorious German armies march through Paris humiliating the French men and women. Christian Diestel and his group of soldiers commit great atrocities in the French countryside as they kill innocent men. Diestel cruelly kills a young French bicyclist and is praised by Hardenburg for doing so.

One of the most important episodes in World War II was the London Blitz or the bomb attack on the city of London. The Germans launched a sudden attack or 'blitz' in the summer of 1940. This attack was aimed at destroying the Royal Air Force of Britain (RAF) and German bombers attacked RAF airfields like Biggin Hill in the south of England and other strategic places such as aircraft factories. This was the 'Battle of Britain'. Between July and September 1940 the skies above the south of England were the scenes of battles between German and British fighter planes. In chapter twenty-two of the novel Shaw provides the reader with a realistic description of the merciless bombing of London and Michael Whitacre is a witness to the barrage. The entire city reeled with shock and disbelief as the German Luftwaffe (Air Force) pelted the city with bombs. All the familiar landmarks of the city like Hyde Park corner, Marble Arch and the Houses of Parliament are ruthlessly bombarded and instantly reduced to ashes. The famous St James Street is one of the first targets as a huge fire engulfs its buildings and devours them greedily. For the residents of London, already facing financial difficulties due to war the air raids were the last straw. In order to make the bombing more terrifying, Shaw sets it against the backdrop of day-to-day happenings in the war ravaged city, as the innocuous inhabitants get caught unawares in the firestorm. The author describes how 'a great many things happened in the city of London' to a large number of its residents many of whom were killed during the first air raids on the city.

One of the most realistic battle scenes of the novel is based on the Battle of Alamein which was fought between Britain and Germany in the deserts of Africa. After being defeated by the British General Montgomery, Hitler's 'desert fox' Rommel was compelled to beat a hasty retreat. This battle marked a significant turning point in the Western Desert Campaign of World War II and success in the battle turned the tide in the North African Campaign. Chapter sixteen of the novel gives a detailed description of this battle between the British and German forces. In the novel, the British catch the German army led by Lieutenant Hardenburg unawares as they launch a sudden attack in the middle of the night. The German forces are completely hemmed in and many members of Hardenburg's unit become cannon fodder for the British artillery. At this juncture Hardenburg and Christian escape on a motorcycle. Shaw provides a macabre but realistic description of the destruction caused by this battle.

Other important historical events like the Normandy Landings and the war in Italy too are mentioned by Shaw. All the three characters in the novel are a part of the action revolving around D day. Noah displays courage during one of the campaigns as he saves the lives of many of his comrades when their unit is ambushed by German forces.

In conclusion it can be said that Shaw's novel is different from that of his contemporaries because he conceived war as taking place at two levels, the level of individual lives and the level of larger culture as he tried to look at combat from the perspective of three men from different backgrounds without losing sight of the war itself as a larger theatre of operations. Shaw's novel is a moral allegory of good versus evil where good triumphs over evil. Noah Ackerman's death is symbolic of the carnage of six million Jews committed by the Nazis during the Second World War, and Diestel's death and Michael's survival are an affirmation of the fact that ultimately 'human beings' are going to rule the world. The concept of morality is an important one in the novel as it emphasizes that every individual must make a moral choice and live by an ethical code of conduct. The novel ends on a positive note, as the author seems to suggest that despite the madness and chaos of modern warfare, there is still hope for man. For every Christian Diestel there are people like Noah and Michael and for every malevolent Colclough there is a benevolent Captain Green providing succour and sustenance, for good and evil are equally balanced in this world. Towards the end of the novel Michael realizes that men like Green with their innate goodness could restore order and sense in the chaotic world:

> "There was nothing, not even the endless depravity and bottomless despair which the Germans had left at the swamp-heart of their dying millennium, which could not be remedied by honest, mechanic's common sense and energy of a decent workman." (*TYL*, 675)

This hope seems to be momentarily shattered when Christian kills Noah, but the latter's vision of a future decent world restores it. The indecent world that Noah had seen has been offset by the decency of Green, the friendship of Michael

Whitacre and the love of his wife Hope. Coming to terms with his Jewish identity was a part of the struggle for self-acceptance and self-awareness and this is the means by which all the world's 'human beings' can be embraced. Although Noah dies in the novel the optimism for a better future continues to linger as Shaw reiterates that in the degenerate and corrupt world human decency will once again reassert itself.

Joseph Heller: *Catch 22*

5

Joseph Heller's first novel *Catch 22*, published in 1961, was hailed by critics as a brilliant piece of work and termed cynically funny, fantastically unique and brutally gruesome. Critics opined that the novel had the power to transform American literature and re-invigorated a fiction, which during the 1950s was reworking with a declining vitality the formulae of earlier years. Heller combined an experimental attitude with a fully contemporary sense of what it meant for a writer to be a radical in the 1960s in American literature. Critics like Norman Podhoretz called Heller "a very good writer with an exceptionally rich talent for comedy" (Podhoretz, 22). Julian Mitchell called *Catch 22* a novel of enormous richness, an art of deep thought and brilliant writing (Mitchell, 32). Frederick Karl praised the novel because it affirmed its faith in survival in an absurd universe (Karl, 164) and Anthony Burgess termed the novel the best satire on the Second World War (Burgess, 53). The novel has also been called "a fantastic and wildly comic parable set on the Italian front in World War II" (Bradbury, 51).

Catch 22 is a novel about the Second Great War but has various other implications too. It not only talks about the war but also talks about the society that came into existence after the war. It deals with the political and social atmosphere of the 1950s and 1960s, the industrial and military expansion of the post-war period and also the paranoia of the Cold War between Russia and America. Heller's novel is an integral part of the novels of social protest written during the 1960s and 1970s. The 1960s have been generally referred to as the Decade of Disillusionment in the history of America. According to sociologist Jim Heath the Kennedy promise turned sour after his assassination. Though the Americans entered the decade with high hopes, it ended with a nation mired in a seemingly endless war with Korea and then with Vietnam. There was a strong note of frustration and despair among the youth of the 1960s and Heller's novel reflects this despair. It was during these decades that American youth truly began to question authority. The Civil Rights Movement, university students and Hippies, all protested against the social and political atmosphere of the period. There is a strong undercurrent of dissent in Heller's novel as well as he remonstrates against the lunacy of war, not only World War II but also other wars that America was waging especially the Vietnam War. Heller's novel protests against the American policy of aggrandizement, the inhumanity of the military bureaucracy and the laissez-faire system of Capitalism where profit motive is the ultimate motive.

While writing *Catch 22*, Heller borrowed from sources as diverse as Kafka, Nathanael West and Dostoevsky (He said in an interview that his chapter titled 'The Eternal City' was inspired by *Crime and Punishment*) in his creation of grotesque and wildly comic characters and episodes. Yossarian, Heller's hero, madly reverses all accepted standards of conduct, in order to preserve the ultimate source of reality, i.e. the self. The stubborn desire for survival in the midst of war is this mad Assyrian's only defense against the dehumanized bureaucracy created by it, and the clinging overpowering conviction of death that is its by product.

Heller's novel is "cynical and stirring and repeatedly talks about human existence and human life" (Kennard, 75). Hailed as a cult novel, *Catch 22* effectively portrays the angst of the postmodernist writer as the world projected by Heller is frenzied, insane and absurd where the individual feels alienated from his environment. *Catch 22* is an integral part of the Literature of the Absurd that has its roots in the Existential philosophy and the view that humans are isolated, alienated and bewildered beings adrift in a meaningless universe. In consonance with these ideas the novel adopts postmodernist techniques like parody and Black Humour, taking a grim look at war without resorting to its realistic description in the tradition of Naturalists like Mailer and Jones. It is important to note that nowhere in the novel is it explicitly mentioned that it is about the Second World War, but the war is there in the backdrop and beneath the humour lies the deadly drama of death and the absurd lunacy of battle. The novel's humour does not alleviate the horror of war but heightens it by contrast and there is much in it that illustrates Charlie Chaplain's dictum that 'humour is playful pain'. Heller is concerned entirely with that thin boundary of the surreal, the borderline between hilarity and horror. Thus he never uses comedy for its own sake; each joke has a wider significance in the intricate pattern so that laughter becomes a prologue for some grotesque revelation. The novel, which proved to be a precursor to the fiction of Donald Barthleme and Thomas Pynchon addresses those who are disaffected, discontented and disaffiliated and yet who want to react to life positively.

The setting of the story is World War II. During the second half of the war, in the year 1944, a soldier named Yossarian is stationed with his air force squadron number 256 on the Island of Pianosa near the Italian coast on the Mediterranean Sea. Yossarian and his comrades from the same squadron Appleby, Doc Daneeka, Orr, Natley, Dunbar, Havermeyer, Hungry Joe and others endure a nightmarish existence caused by war, military bureaucracy and violence. They are considered to be inhuman resources by their blindly ambitious superior officers. The novel opens with a number of officers malingering in a hospital; one of these is Yossarian himself who is engaged in censoring all modifiers out of enlisted men's letters and signing the censor's name as 'Washington Irving' and sometimes as 'Irving Washington'. On some days he removes all articles from these letters and at other times he removes the salutations. The cast of characters introduced to us in the novel is insanely funny. A soldier named Dunbar is engaged in "pursuing tedious conversation with boring Texans in order to increase his life-span by making time pass slowly" (*Catch 22*, 16), yet another character called Orr "stores horse chestnuts in his cheeks to give himself a look of innocence", a character named Appleby insists that he has flies in his eyes, while another, Hungry Joe has recurring nightmares—this cast of characters is grotesque and their malingering reflects their ennui and the fact that many of them are in the hospital to avoid combat.

The squadron, which is made up of these crazy men is thrown thoughtlessly into brutal combat situations and bombing runs in which it is more important for the squadron members to capture good aerial photographs of explosions than to destroy their targets. The superior officers continually raise the number of missions that each member of the squadron is required to fly before being sent home, so that no one is ever sent home. Yossarian's story forms the core of the novel, so most events are reflected through his point of view. He takes the whole war personally rather than being swayed by national ideals or abstract principles like duty and patriotism. He is furious that his life is in constant danger through no fault of his own and that he has to continually fly missions against the enemy. He has a strong desire to live and is determined to survive despite all odds. As a result, he pretends to be insane and spends a large part of the time at the hospital faking various illnesses in order to avoid going to combat missions.

As the novel progresses, Yossarian is troubled by the memory of Snowden, a soldier who had died in his arms on a mission making Yossarian lose all desire to participate in the war. He is placed in ridiculous, tragic and even absurd circumstances as he sees his comrades like Natley, Dunbar, Dobbs, Kid Sampson and others die during dangerous combat missions. Many others 'disappear' or are reported missing in action as the ruthless superior officers, the Colonels and Generals volunteer their men for the most perilous battles. He protests against this inhumanity by appearing nude just when he is to receive a medal and then again by sitting on a tree during Snowden's funeral. He even poisons his own squadron and moves the bomb line to Bologna but the authorities despite taking notice of his protests go on raising the number of missions in order to enhance their own reputation. Colonel Cathcart a senior officer for instance wants to get his picture in the *Saturday Evening Post* by raising the number of missions continually, from forty to eighty during the course of the novel.

Although Yossarian's story forms the nucleus, there are a number of other stories related to other characters in the novel. An important story revolves around 'Natley's Whore', and her kid sister whom Yossarian tries to rescue in Rome. Natley is a young pilot who is in love with a prostitute in Rome and is killed during the battle over La Spezia. When the news of his death reaches this prostitute she is devastated and blames Yossarian for his demise and even stabs him with a knife in anger. The story of Orr's escape to Sweden is an important event in the novel. Orr, a character who appears to be slightly mad keeps landing his plane into the sea and giggles helplessly when he is rescued from the water. Ultimately it is discovered that Orr was practicing his strategy for escape. Another story follows the rise of the black market empire of Milo, the squadron's Mess Hall officer. Milo owns a syndicate in which he borrows military planes and pilots to transport food between various points in Europe, making massive profits from his sales and although he claims that 'everyone has a share', in the syndicate, this promise proves to be false. Milo's enterprise flourishes nonetheless and communities all over Europe revere him.

The novel draws to a close as Yossarian, lying in hospital, injured by the knife attack made on him by Natley's Whore refuses to fly any more missions. He wanders on the war torn streets of Rome, encountering every possible human horror from rape to disease to murder, and all the devastation caused by war. He is eventually arrested for being in Rome without a pass and is hauled up before his superior officers Cathcart and Korn who offer him a choice of either facing a court martial or being released and sent home with an honourable discharge. However, there is only one condition and that is that in order to be released, he must approve of Cathcart and Korn and support their policy, which requires all the men in the squadron to fly eighty missions. Although he is tempted by the offer, Yossarian realizes that to agree would be to endanger the lives of innocent men. He chooses another way out, and decides to desert the army and flee to neutral Sweden. In doing so he turns his back on the dehumanizing cold machinery of the military, rejects the insanity of war and strives for a future in which he is in control of his own life and also to some extent the lives of his fellow human beings.

The title of the novel itself is significant. Catch 22 became an integral part of the English language after Heller's novel was published in 1961. If it is simply defined the phrase means a 'no win situation'. This situation is one where the individual has a choice but no choice leads to success. For example, if an executioner offers the condemned the choice of dying by being hanged, shot or poisoned, all choices lead to death and the condemned is in a no-win situation. Thus in the novel war created by the military bureaucracy is a no win situation. Catch 22 makes an appearance several times during the course of the novel and has different interpretations. It is the governing principle of the entire novel and is the 'law' that is defined in various ways throughout the novel. Catch 22 takes many forms but the central one is that you don't have to fly any more missions if you're crazy, but you have to ask first and anyone who wants to get out of combat duty isn't crazy.

The first time this law makes its appearance is in Chapter five, when Yossarian discovers that it is possible to be grounded on the basis of insanity. Always looking for a way out Yossarian claims that he is insane only to find out that by claiming that he is insane he has proved that he is obviously sane—a sane person would only avoid flying bombing missions.

> "There was only one catch and that was Catch 22, which specified that a concern for one's own safety in the face of dangers that were real and immediate was the process of a rational mind. Orr was crazy and could be grounded. All he had to do was ask and as soon as he did, he would no longer be crazy and would have to fly more missions. He would be crazy to fly more mission and sane if he did not, but if he was sane he had to fly them. If he flew them he was crazy and didn't have to; but if he didn't want to he was sane and had to. Yossarian was moved very deeply by the absolute simplicity of this clause of Catch 22 and let

> out a respectful whistle.... Yossarian saw it clearly in all its spinning reasonableness. There was an elliptical precision about its perfect pairs of parts that was graceful and shocking, like good modern art, and at times Yossarian was not sure that he saw it at all, just the way he was never quite sure about good modern art or about flies one saw in Appleby's eyes." (*Catch 22*, 52, and 62-63)

The 'catch' of Catch 22 traps Yossarian in a hopeless situation. He cannot avoid flying combat missions by pretending to be insane because an insane person would not know about the dangers of war and the risk of flying bombing missions. At another place in the novel Catch 22 is defined as an illegal 'law' and yet it is the governing principle of the military bureaucracy. Heller shows that this law is a ridiculous one, for instance it says that fire personnel must always be on the airfield when planes returning from bombing missions land. Thus, in the novel firemen leave a blaze they are attempting to control at the hospital, just in order to obey this rule thereby endangering several lives. Catch 22 is therefore composed of systems, rules and commands that have no meaningful relation to one another as they are whimsical, capricious, arbitrary and ridiculous. Catch 22 is any paradoxical, circular reasoning that catches its victim in its illogic and serves those who have made the law.

Catch 22 gives the army absolute and total power. It is a law that says what it commands is right because it is commanded and the illogical must be done because the command says it is logical. This law is used by the army to bind the individual to only those possibilities, which strengthen the system, rather than the individual. Heller while criticizing the army calls Catch 22 the untouchable power that has usurped man's control over his own life, and handed it over to an institution, which manufactures fatal and incredible death traps, ensnaring the individual, making escape impossible. Thomas Blues is of the opinion that "at the heart of Catch 22 lies betrayal of decent values, the requirement that one sells one's soul to survive" (Blues, 65). Yossarian realizes that Catch 22 is the most powerful force in the set up of the army and is a trap, which holds human beings captive and forces them to surrender their individuality becoming automatons or replaceable parts of the military machinery, which is fighting the war. Yossarian is able to escape the tenacious grip of Catch 22 by deserting. The novel reveals that Catch 22 not only governs the army, but has its unrelenting grip on society as well. Joseph Epstein is of the opinion that "it is the great social tautology that imprisons every individual" (Epstein, 1).

In Chapter thirty nine, Catch 22 reveals itself in Rome devastated and ruined by the war. When Yossarian visits this city an old woman sitting among the ruins informs him that the Italian military police is harassing the residents of the town. When Yossarian asks her the reason behind this harassment she says 'Catch 22':

> "Catch 22 says they have a right to do anything we can't stop them from doing. The soldiers with the hard white hats and clubs...all that the men kept saying was Catch 22, Catch 22. 'Didn't they show it to you?' Yossarian demanded stamping about in anger and distress 'Didn't you make them read it?' 'They don't have to show us Catch 22', the old woman answered 'The law says they don't have to...the law of Catch 22'." (*Catch 22*, 514)

This is the ultimate horror of Catch 22 because it connotes a world where values have declined and "power is the ultimate morality" (Olderman, 94). Catch 22 is Heller's illustration of the irrational nature of the world and any attempt to argue logically and reasonably ends in a paradox. The law thus extends beyond the army and has become the principle of life itself. Catch 22 makes its final appearance when Yossarian is hauled up before Cathcart and Korn who are going to promote him, give him another medal and send him home a hero, but there is a 'catch', that is Yossarian will have to strike a despicable and self-serving deal with them.

Like Catch 22, the war is shown to be absurd as well. Heller strips away heroism from war revealing that sentiments like duty and patriotism are mere words with no meaning. He looks at war in a very unsentimental manner, stripping all romantic pretences away from combat and replacing visions of glory and honour with a kind of nightmarish comedy of violence and madness. Although he does not mention Nazism until the very end of the novel, he calls the war a 'fraud' and emphasizes the horrible meaninglessness of armed conflict. None of the soldiers in Yossarian's 256th squadron find the war heroic, glorious or romantic. Most of the men in the squadron are mechanically obeying the orders of superior officers not owing to any patriotism but in the desperate hope that one day the flying missions would finally come to an end and they would be sent home. These soldiers have no burning desire to defeat Hitler and the evil of fascism. Most men (like Yossarian) would like to get out of combat duty but cannot change the situation because the war has numbed their senses to such an extent that they have stopped responding to the drama of death and violence and even accuse Yossarian of having 'survival anxieties'.

There is nothing gallant and wonderful about the death of the pilots of the squadron stationed at Pianosa. The death of Natley, Dunbar and Kid Sampson are extremely tragic. In fact, the death of Snowden is the most tragic event in the novel and also Yossarian's most intimate experience of death. When Snowden and Heller's hero were flying in the same aircraft during a mission their plane was hit and Snowden was injured but it was mistakenly believed that Yossarian had been hit and people called through the intercom to help the bombardier who was Yossarian. His comrade Dobbs cried out in an anguished tone: 'help him, help him, Dobbs sobbed...the bombardier'. To which Yossarian replied 'I'm the bombardier. I'm all right...and Snowden lay dying in the back' (*Catch 22*, 552).

Snowden kept saying that he was cold and Yossarian did all that he could to help him by making him comfortable and putting a tourniquet on a shrapnel wound in his leg. He even searched through the first aid kit for morphine, which could have relieved Snowden of his pain only to find the kit empty because Milo the mercenary mess hall officer of the squadron had appropriated the entire supply of the drug for his syndicate. However, Snowden had been seriously wounded inside his flak suit and ultimately succumbed to his injury despite Yossarian's best effort to save him. Heller provides the reader a graphic description of the soldier's death: "Snowden was wounded inside his flak suit...he turned back weakly to Snowden, whose breath had grown softer and more rapid and whose face had grown paler. He wondered how in the world to begin to save him" (*Catch 22*, 553-54).

Snowden's death is perhaps the only dramatic event and a description of death during combat though there is nothing heroic about this episode. His death is presented incrementally; we are given glimpses here and there throughout the novel, but never the complete dramatization of it until the penultimate chapter, when Yossarian is lying wounded in the hospital. According to Thomas Blues, Snowden's death, which is repeated several times in the novel, does not really occur until the moment when Yossarian recognizes its true meaning and significance that is the meaninglessness and absurdity of war. Once he learns to read 'the message in Snowden's entrails', he attempts to respond appropriately, in various ways to his comrade's death. He discards his blood-covered uniform and receives a medal nude and even attends Snowden's funeral in the nude thereby displaying his anger, despair and frustration at the lunacy of war. Thus, Heller's novel upholds the idea that in the mad, impersonal killing of modern warfare valour is a joke and men die under the false illusion that it is a noble gesture to give up one's life for one's country. The assumptions of *Catch 22* are that courage, bravery and love for one's country and other human virtues are all a hideous cover up for the urge towards self-advancement and a desire to be powerful. The author opines: "Men went mad and were awarded with medals. All over the world, boys on every side of the bomb line were laying down their lives for what they had been told was their country" (*Catch 22*, 25).

Heller believes that suffering, cruelty and death are the byproducts of war and he subtly reveals this in the novel without dramatizing the anguish of his characters. A single chapter, the darkest in the novel titled 'The Eternal City' is devoted to the description of devastation caused by the war and it describes the war-wrecked city of Rome. Yossarian visits this city after Natley's death and encounters tableau after tableau of cruelty, destruction, hünger and poverty. A nursing mother holds an infant in tattered rags while an emaciated, barefoot boy struggles against the cold. In another part of the city, a woman is raped. Yossarian encounters the horrifying scene of a man whipping his dog, a sight reminiscent of the famous scene from *Crime and Punishment* where Raskolnikov dreams of the whipping of a horse. Sick in spirit, Yossarian goes back to the officers' apartments where he finds that one of his comrades Aarfy has brutally raped and killed the officers' young maid Michaela. When Yossarian expresses his distress and horror over the death of the innocent girl Aarfy callously replies: "Oh I had to do that after I raped her. I couldn't very well let her go around saying bad things about us, could I?" (*Catch 22*, 525). Heller seems to suggest that the bestiality of war turns human beings into beasts themselves.

Yossarian's mental anguish is revealed to the reader not through a realistic description but in a humorous manner, which nevertheless disturbs the reader and one begins to sympathize with the pilot's predicament. After witnessing so much distress and remembering his own suffering too Heller's hero finally decides to turn his back on this mad war torn scenario by deserting and walking backwards with his gun on his hip musing that "If I give up my life now, it wouldn't be for my country. It would be for Cathcart and Korn.... From now on I'm thinking only of me" (*Catch 22*, 561).

In contemporary literature the concept of identity has become an important issue with several postmodernist writers portraying the angst of the individual who has lost his 'true self' and feels alienated from his environment. Drawing upon the theories of psychoanalysts contemporary writers have discussed concepts such as 'fragmented', 'dislocated' and 'schizoid' identities in their works. For Heller the issue of identity is an important one as well for he realizes that the impact of war on an individual causes a loss of identity. It is in keeping with this idea that Heller has created mad and outlandish characters who are caricatures of the Dickensian type and are merely cardboard figures having no individual identity. These characters are introduced to us through short explanatory paragraphs which appear to sum up their personalities in a few adjectives but which provide no clues for their exhaustive analysis. They may have names, heredity, profession and faces but they do not seem to be real. For instance an officer of the 256th squadron is called 'Major Major Major'. He has no identity as a person and is identified only by his rank—that of a Major.

At one point in the novel Yossarian tries to change his identity by pretending to be a dying officer whose parents visit him in the hospital. Even the parents of the officer fail to recognize the fact that they are meeting a stranger and not their own son. In another section of the novel Yossarian and Dunbar discover that they can change identities by changing hospital beds. The army has crushed the individuality of these soldiers and they have become 'parts' of the war machine. Heller repeatedly uses the word 'disappear' while talking about a character. Disappear not only means 'missing in action' or 'dead', but also refers to the loss of identity that these characters undergo. Most of the characters in *Catch 22* have lost their sanity and are reduced to ridiculous figures. For instance there is Orr who stuffs crab apples in his cheeks, giggles helplessly each time Yossarian makes an attempt to start a conversation with him and crash-lands into water on a regular basis. Orr ultimately escapes the chaos of war when he flees to Sweden. Yet another character introduced to the reader is Hungry Joe, the miserable pilot who is on the brink of collapse due to incessant flying: "Hungry Joe could no longer stand the strain of waiting for shipping orders and crumbled promptly into ruin each time he finished another tour of duty" (*Catch 22*, 72).

The 'bureaucratically dead' Doc Daneeka (actually he is dead only on paper and in the records of the army) is a doctor who responds to all his patients' complaints by telling them about his own troubles. Doc Daneeka is a decent man whose rise to financial security has been cruelly destroyed after he is drafted into the army and he never tires of complaining about his financial losses. Aarfy is another of Yossarian's comrades who keeps smiling for no reason at all. All the other characters

Havermeyer, Dunbar, Appleby, Mcwatt, Dobbs, Chief Whitehafloat are unaware of the death and destruction around them and thus appear to be insane. This is because as 'parts' of the war machine they have witnessed so much destruction that they have become numb towards violence and pain. For instance, in one of the episodes in the novel, Yossarian is hit during a mission and cries for help, Aarfy who is with him cannot hear his anguished cries because flying several missions and witnessing excessive bloodshed have benumbed him. In fact none of the characters can hear his cries and think that he is crazy when he declares that people are trying to kill him.

In *The Naked and the Dead* Norman Mailer criticizes war as an incubator of totalitarianism, which gives birth to regimentation and creates the institution of the army. Heller too adopts a similar stance, looking upon the army as an organization, which springs from the necessity of war, stifles individualism and makes survival impossible. The military establishment is perceived as a greater threat to human life than the war itself. This criticism of the military bureaucracy is forcefully presented in the novel. The military establishment, which claims to be a protection against chaos of war, threatens human life more insidiously than battle itself. Peter G. Jones is of the opinion that the establishment that is fighting the war destroys sanity, life and the human spirit (Jones, 81). The establishment, which in the name of reason, patriotism and righteousness has seized control over man's life, reduced the individual to 'nothingness' and created a regimented society, proves to be the real terror of the novel.

To begin with, Heller looks upon the army as 'the enemy within'. Not only does he talk about enemies across no man's land and vast stretches of water i.e. the Germans or Japanese, the Rome-Tokyo-Berlin Axis but also about enemies within one's own country. The enemy is anybody who is endangering survival and there are references to pernicious enemies, the enemy within. "The enemy is anybody who's going to get you killed no matter which side he's on" (*Catch 22*, 161). According to this logic, Yossarian is surrounded on all sides by hostile forces and his enemies are distinguished less by their nationality and more by their ability to get him killed. Thus, he feels a 'blind electric rage' against the Germans whenever they hurl flak at his aircraft and feels an equally profound hatred for those of his own countrymen who exercise an arbitrary power over his life and well-being. These are superior officers like Colonel Cathcart who go on raising the number of missions even if they touch six thousand and continue endangering the lives of the officers. The enemy is officers like General Peckham who volunteer the men for the most dangerous of missions in order to get themselves promoted. These are Yossarian's antagonists and all are identified by their totally mechanical attitude towards human life. The enemy is thus very much here implying thereby that Yossarian's own countrymen are his enemies.

Heller directs his attack against the officers of the army who are referred to as 'the military bureaucracy', in the novel and displays many unpalatable aspects of it. He had participated in the war and the novel is based on his personal experience. He had interacted with the officers of the army and the novel reveals that the bureaucracy is made up of officers who are ambitious, jealous, engaged in petty quarrelling and victimization of their colleagues and juniors. Shedding light on the functioning of the bureaucracy Heller reveals through numerous examples a cadre of officers who are hypocrites and who display a flagrant disregard and insensitivity towards human life.

One of the senior officers of the 256th squadron stationed at Pianosa is Colonel Cathcart who is highly ambitious. In chapter nineteen he is described as a "slick, successful, slipshod unhappy man of thirty-six...an industrious, intense, dedicated military technician who calculated day and night in the service of himself" (*Catch 22*, 240). Cathcart desperately wants to be promoted to the rank of a General because being fiercely competitive, he can measure himself only in relation to others. He is delighted about the fact that he is a Colonel at such a young age while other, older officers hold a lower rank, but becomes extremely upset when he learns of a General even younger than himself. Besides wanting a promotion, this egocentric, over ambitious officer desperately wants his photograph to be published in the *Saturday Evening Post* and to achieve this end he has tripled the required number of missions that the men of his squadron must fly before they are relieved from combat duty. Cathcart's policies result in a large number of casualties but the ruthless Colonel pays no attention to the lives being lost. If one pilot dies another would replace him. But the missions had to go on because these missions were feathers in his cap.

Victimization is an all-pervasive phenomenon in the military bureaucracy. Heller shows us this through the character of Captain Black. Black is one of the most vindictive characters in the novel. He is extremely jealous of Major Major because the post of squadron commander has been given to Major Major instead of Captain Black. Vengeance against Major Major precipitates Captain Black's Glorious Loyalty Oath when he accuses Major Major of being a Communist and then makes everyone in the squadron sign the Oath disclaiming Communism. Major Major however was never allowed to sign thus putting his loyalty to question. Through the Glorious Loyalty Oath Black not only victimizes Major Major but also other members of the squadron. Initially combat personnel had to sign the Oath in order to get parachutes and other equipment required for flying. But soon the men had to sign the Oath and disclaim Communism to get knives, forks, spoons and even food. Condemning this kind of persecution and victimization, Heller states in the novel:

> "Almost overnight the Glorious Loyalty Oath Crusade was in full flower. All the enlisted men and officers on combat duty had to sign a loyalty oath to get their map cases from the intelligence tent...they signed a loyalty oath to get their pay from the finance officer, to have their haircut by Italian barbers." (*Catch 22,* 147)

Another instance of victimization occurs when the CID officers subject the Chaplain of the squadron, Chaplain Tappman to intimidating interrogation. These investigative authorities are looking for the mysterious 'Washington Irving' who has been censoring letters of the members of the squadron. As has been mentioned earlier it was Yossarian signing as Washington Irving. The authorities of course are unaware of this fact and unable to find the real culprit they arrest and persecute the innocent Chaplain.

The novel reveals most of the officers of the 256th squadron to be hypocrites. Lieutenant Colonel Korn is an amoral hypocrite who pretends to be Cathcart's loyal, indispensable ally but secretly feels contemptuous towards him. He tries to manipulate Cathcart to his own advantage. Colonel Cathcart is a religious hypocrite. In the *Saturday Evening Post* he reads about a bomber group in England that prays before each mission. He asks Chaplain Tappman to try the same tactic in order to get him some publicity, though he is neither concerned with God, nor spirituality and religion. The elitist Cathcart's plan however fails when the Chaplain insists that the pilots of the squadron must also be included in the prayer service. Colonel Cathcart is most upset to learn that the enlisted men pray to the same God as officers: "What are you talking about? You mean they pray to the same god as we do? 'Yes sir' 'And he listens'? I think so Sir" (*Catch 22,* 248). The hypocrite that Cathcart is, he immediately decides to abandon the prayer sessions.

Since war is an irrational phenomenon, Heller believes that the organization fighting the war too is largely governed by irrationality. What happens to one of the pilots Clevinger is an example of this illogicality. Clevinger, an intellectual, and a man of reason makes an attempt to confront the irrationality of the military with pure rationality but fails. Lieutenant Scheisskopf lodges imaginary complaints against Clevinger and then as a member of his Action Board simultaneously performs the role of judge, prosecutor and defending officer and victimizes him. The army with its absurd reasoning declares Doc Daneeka 'dead' because he is dead according to the records of the army when in actuality he is very much alive. Doc Daneeka was supposedly a member of the crew that died during a plane crash. 'Bureaucratically dead', he is a walking corpse, on paper, and his fellow men constantly remind him: "You're dead Sir'...that's probably the reason you always feel so cold" (*Catch 22,* 432).

The military bureaucracy created by the war is not only guided by irrationality but is also a monstrous organization totally insensitive to human life. Corporal Whitecomb the Chaplain's assistant displays a flagrant disregard for human life. Whitecomb unimaginatively and insensitively devises a form letter to take care of the growing casualties resulting from Cathcart's policies. The letter reads: "Dear Mrs, Mr, Miss or Mr and Mrs: words cannot express the deep profound grief I experienced when your husband, son, father or brother was killed, wounded or reported missing in action." Thus death becomes merely routine paperwork for these officers. The attention paid to the 'soldier in white' is also an instance of the bureaucracy's absurdity and lack of sensitivity. The soldier in white is merely a body of cast, attended assiduously by the nurses who devotedly dust the cast and polish the metal pipes through which the same fluid is poured and re-poured. No one knows whether the soldier in white is male or female, black or white. The soldier's limbs are pinioned in air by lead weights. Nurse Cramer tells Yossarian his 'leg belongs to the U.S. government'. The soldier in white reveals the absence of spirit in the bureaucratic setup. The authorities of the military establishment will never pay heed to living creatures like the men in the 256th squadron. The military bureaucracy is a creation of the war yet Heller like Mailer, expresses a fear that the army may continue to remain powerful even after the war and this trend may become dangerous for society.

Catch 22 is a scathing critique of Capitalism and the American greed where profit motive is the ultimate motive be it war or peace. Heller wonders how human beings could even think of making profits during a situation like war and portrays a society gone completely awry.

Brian Way is of the opinion that one of the most important strands in the American novel since 1900 has been the criticism of American materialism and obsession with money (Way, 253). Heller's novel also continues in the same tradition and attacks Capitalism through Milo Minderbinder, a war profiteer and black marketeer. Heller's views on the American capitalist society of the 1960s and 70s are in conjunction with views expressed by postmodernist thinker Guy Debord who uses terms like 'spectacle' and 'commodification' to describe the post-war American society. Debord was a spokesman for a radical group of artists and social critics known as the Situationist International. Centred in France and most active in the 1960s, they saw consumer and media culture as an insidious form of oppression. Debord is of the view that Capitalism transforms the world by turning everything including social relations into a 'spectacle' and excessive 'commodification' turns human beings into passive spectators of life (Ward, 220). This happens when the unscrupulous Milo uses a situation like war to make profits while the members of his squadron watch helplessly, unable to change the situation. As the Mess Hall officer of 256th squadron he creates a syndicate called 'M and M Enterprises' which controls the black market. A promising entrepreneur but a businessman without a conscience, his slogan is 'What's good for M and M Enterprises is good for the country.'

The corrupt Milo parlays his position as a Mess Hall officer into personal direction of M and M Enterprises, controlling all sorts of goods and services from fresh eggs to prostitutes. Anxious to turn the war into a business venture, Milo's syndicate corners world market on all available foodstuffs from Lebanese cedar to Swiss cheese, Spanish oranges even Dutch Tulips and Egyptian cotton which he then sells to the army mess halls at huge profits. His planes arrive daily from such markets as Liberia, London and Karachi. He is extremely successful and his business and political connections make him Mayor of every town in Sicily, Vice-Shah of Oran, Caliph of Baghdad, Imam of Damascus and Sheikh of Araby. He insists that he operates a 'legitimate' business in the American way, for each member of the squadron is a shareholder in the syndicate as well but the profits are all plowed back into the business. He makes huge profits from the battle of Orvieto, helps the Allies plan the bombing of a highway bridge at Orvieto and even conducts the attack for them. On the other hand he agrees with the Germans too to defend the same bridge with antiaircraft fire, bargaining for cost plus six percent from each side and also a 'merit bonus' of one thousand dollars from the Germans for each plane shot down. Having arranged all the details the wily Milo has no trouble convincing both sides to furnish their own men and equipment and though lives are lost during this battle he nevertheless makes a huge profit.

One of Milo's most callous actions is appropriating large quantities of morphine for his syndicate. When Snowden is injured and Yossarian searches for a pain killer in the first-aid kit to relieve Snowden's pain he finds instead of morphine a ruthless message on a printed slip of paper: 'What's good for M&M Enterprises is good for the country.' Milo's slogan is reminiscent of what Charles E. Wilson, Eisenhower's Secretary for Defence and former president of General Motors had said to the American people about General Motors 'What's good for General Motors is good for the country.' Heller reveals that the ruthless Milo has carried this slogan to an extreme, manipulating it for selfish ends and for making profits. Milo's heartless action results in Snowden's painful death due to lack of medical aid. Ironically, the death of human beings seems to be 'good' for M and M enterprises.

Although Milo trades with the whole world, he does not trade with Russia because of their being a Communist country. However, he has no compunctions about trading with the Germans even though the Allies were at war with them. This consideration is purely mercenary as is Milo's contention that the Germans are not the enemy. He tells Yossarian:

> ..."Sure we are at war with them. But the Germans are also members in good standing of the syndicate and it is my job to protect their rights as shareholders. Maybe they did start the war, and maybe they are killing millions of people, but they pay their bills a lot more promptly than some allies of ours I could name. Don't you understand that I have to respect the sanctity of my contract with Germany." (*Catch 22*, 252)

Without any qualms of conscience he enters into a contract with Germany to bomb and strafe his own targets and airfields with planes from his squadron, justifying his action with the strong cry 'what's good for the syndicate is good for the country'. This happens when Milo's cash flow is trapped due to the purchase of the entire Egyptian cotton crop and he is unable to sell the cotton in the market. Heller criticizes the Capitalist principle that can allow Milo to glibly overlook Nazi crimes against human life.

Despite the fact that many of his own men die when he bombs his own squadron and it is felt that Milo 'had indeed gone too far', he continues to be admired and respected by the American people even though grudgingly by those who had lost loved ones in the bombing and strafing. A successful businessman Milo's books show a substantial profit in keeping with the American Capitalist ethos and the rules of the laissez-faire economy where profit is the ultimate motive.

This profit motive makes insensitive blackmarketeers like Milo thrive, for human life for them is just a commodity readily expendable when ample reimbursement can be made. Brian Way draws a parallel between Milo and Cottard, the black marketeer in Camu's *The Plague* where Cottard takes maximum advantage of the plague and is unhappy and in despair when the contagion dies down. Similarly Milo profits from the war, does not wish it to end even though it causes death and unhappiness.

Heller is of the view that the Protestant work ethic responsible for the material progress of America seems to have run wild becoming life negating and creating an absurd society. Yet men like Milo flourish in this absurd world, exploit absurd institutions, use specious reasoning and speak the language of Catch 22. Heller criticizes Capitalism and expresses the view that avarice has led to a loss of basic values among people like Milo Minderbinder, individuals who treat friends and foes alike and can only think of personal gain even in the most adverse circumstances.

Structurally, the novel is a typically postmodernist text sans a beginning, middle and end. It is episodic and comprises a series of loosely related tangential stories in no particular chronological order. The structure, chaotic and zigzag, seems to emphasize the chaos of the war. However, critics like Clinton S.

Burhans do see unifying elements in the novel, arguing that a basic narrative structure holds the novel together. Burhans opines:

> "This structure can be visualized as a kind of a narrative tree with the trunk comprising primarily of the main plot—Yossarian's efforts to get off flying status either by achieving the required number of missions or by having himself declared insane. There are two subplots, the struggle between Peckham and Dreedle for command of the wing and that of Milo's syndicate. Around this trunk grow in abundance two kinds of branches, arranged for visual convenience one on either side. Those on the left whether simple references or detailed episodes are expository flashbacks made once for informational purposes or repeated for thematic effect. Those on the right are foreshadowing flashbacks which link the different chapters." (Burhans, 240)

Burhans is of the opinion that a structural pattern emerges in the novel and Heller has distributed sufficient elements of continuity and transition to give the work a controlling structural design beneath its kaleidoscopic surface. Contrary to the general perception, this critic believes that there is actually no formlessness in the novel and Yossarian's fight against the authorities to save his own life has a definite pattern of growth despite the fluctuation between distant past and immediate present.

Heller, himself shedding light on the structure of the novel says in an interview that 9/10th of *Catch 22* is organized around three combat missions—the mission to Avignon, the mission to Bologna and the mission to Ferrara. The first mission is the main one. The whole novel is a series of events that either deal with the missions or are outgrowths of events that happened on the mission (Sale, 65). The missions have already occurred before the time of the opening chapter and keep recurring throughout the novel. Heller continually and consciously follows this pattern of recurrence. Yossarian flies over the bridge at

Ferrara twice, Snowden's death keeps recurring (until Yossarian comprehends the real meaning of his death) the soldier in white appears twice and the Chaplain has his deja-vu susceptibilities—this is a pattern. Heller however admits in the interview that 4/5ths of the novel is conceived in chaotic terms.

Jean Kennard is of the opinion that Heller's vision of the world in *Catch 22* is similar to that of Existentialist philosophers like Jean Paul Sartre and Albert Camus (Kennard, 77). The Existentialists believe that the world is violent, chaotic, sans religion, morality and above all reason. In fact after the war the world had become meaningless and Man's attempt to seek any meaning became a futile endeavour. Since reason and language, the tools for discovering the purpose of existence and describing the world had become useless, Man's relationship with this topsy-turvy world had become 'Absurd'. Human beings had been robbed of a meaningful existence and were trapped by their environment as all escape routes were closed. Camus and Sartre believe that modern Man feels alienated by his environment and is continuously searching for a sense of 'self' in a ruthless and hostile world. When Man discovers these facts about his condition he experiences what Sartre calls 'nausea' and what other Existentialist thinkers term as 'metaphysical anguish'.

The war torn world of *Catch 22* is similar to the world portrayed by Existentialist thinkers in their works. This is a violent, chaotic, absurd and hollow place where the military bureaucracy, has a tenacious grip on the lives of the soldiers. Yossarian, trapped by this monstrous organization is like the Existential hero a 'quester' who is continuously searching for 'meaning' in this insane universe. For instance he wants to know why people are trying to kill him and what is the purpose of the war that has claimed so many lives. Apart from Yossarian, the Chaplain too experiences this absurd predicament. He feels: "Terrifying sudden movements when objects, concepts and even people that the chaplain had lived with all his life took on an unfamiliar and irregular aspect that he had never seen before" (*Catch 22*, 262).

In an environment where philosophical ideas, traditional morality and religion are useless all man has left is his own body. Frederick Karl is of the opinion that "the individual has the right to seek survival...one's own substance is infinitely more precious than any cause" (Karl, 168). There is no talk of love or even close friendship in *Catch 22* for Heller supports individual human life throughout the novel. The pleasures of life too are purely physical—food, liquor, sex and the real horror of physical pain and ultimately death. Since Heller gives so much importance to human life in his novel he believes that valid action is possible for human beings and a Man trapped by his environment can escape from it. There is even the suggestion of a sane universe, which Sweden may represent; perhaps it is only a state of mind rather than a real place, although Orr has at least reportedly reached Sweden. It is this stubborn desire to hold on to his sense of self that makes Yossarian fight for survival in the lunatic world of *Catch 22*. His environment is certainly hostile, he is ensnared by it but he makes a moral choice and ultimately deserts, choosing survival and life over death and the illogicality of war.

Owing to his desertion critics have called Yossarian a coward, an amoralist and a traitor and his decision has been looked upon as patriotically and morally wrong. However, he deserts not because he is a coward but because he comes to the conclusion that his continued participation in the war would have little effect beyond making things easier for the selfish men who commanded him. Neither he nor his squadron mates or his country would be the primary beneficiary. Thus, Yossarian acts as a responsible individual who does not compromise his integrity by stubbornly refusing to support the life negating policies of Cathcart and Korn. Frederick Karl terms Yossarian's decision as an act of 'good faith'. In an interview Heller stated:

> "He has deluded himself into thinking that all he wants to do is to survive. He has the opportunity and accepts it in despair. In the hospital he finds that he can't accept it because there is a moral life inside him. As scared as he is of dying, he doesn't want to live if it has to be in terms of calling those colonels by their first

> names. Being on a first name basis with the Establishment. He would rather be a fugitive. It was an awesome decision." (Sale, 73)

According to Walter McDonald in making a 'separate peace' Yossarian follows the tradition adopted by other 'deserters' of American fiction like Natty Bumpo, Hester Prynne, Huck Finn, Frederick Henry and John Andrews who upon hearing "a distant drummer, light out for a different territory" (McDonald, 14).

Heller rejected Naturalistic and realistic techniques and adopted the postmodernist Absurdist style of writing in order to convey his horror of war. Heller reveals how language can no longer be used as a means of communication in a war-ravaged world as words lose their meaning and only increase the confusion. In this respect, Yossarian and other characters in the novel have experiences similar to those of Roquentin in Sartre's novel *Nausea*. While travelling on a trolley car Roquentin suddenly loses the context of his situation, as the buildings outside rather than the streetcar seem to be moving. This terrifies him and he tries to stabilize his experience with language but realizes that words have failed him and things are divorced from their names. In *Catch 22* words have lost their original connections to things they represent, and W. Holbling calls this the "discontinuity between the signifier and the signified and the communicative dilemma that results from this disruption" (Holbling, 58). Since words are redundant, Heller appears to be playing with language in the novel and in the first chapter we find Yossarian making a game of censoring letters declaring one day 'death to all modifiers', the next declaring 'a war on all articles' and finally blacking out everything except 'a', 'an' and 'the' Heller describes Yossarian's action thus:

> "Death to all modifiers, he declared one day and out of every letter that passed through his hands went every adverb and every adjective. The next day he made a war on articles. He reached a much higher plane of creativity the following day when he blacked out everything in the letters but a, an, the." (*Catch 22*, 14)

At first this act seems terrible: the letters are the men's only way of communicating with their loved ones and Yossarian destroys that line of communication. However, in the chaotic world of *Catch 22* language has no communicative power. As Snowden lay dying in the back of the plane all Yossarian could think of saying was 'there, there' all over again. Faced with the realities of death and absurdity of circumstances, language seems unable to communicate any sort of reassurance to Snowden. Even officers like General Peckham who lay great stress on small matters of taste and style while communicating through letters have lost all sense of what the words mean.

Contemporary writers like Barth and Pynchon perceive external reality as an illusion and focus on inner reality. One trademark of this inner reality has been a psychological sense of time that does not follow the chronological and causal sequence. *Catch 22* disrupts linear time and opens 'in the middle of things' or what is called 'media res'. It begins in 1944 when Yossarian is in the hospital and meets the Chaplain. The events are not in chronological order and the action moves back and forth in time which itself seems to be out of joint. Critics have pointed out that the time shown in the novel is not clock time but psychological time in keeping with the theories of Bergson and Proust. Psychological time refers to the passage of time that passes in the mind of the characters, rather than the external world. The idea of time being out of joint is further emphasized when the Chaplain has his 'déjà vu' susceptibilities and is convinced that he is experiencing certain events twice. The author creates temporal disorder through the use of flashback as the action swings back and forth. Most of the action in the novel is depicted in flashbacks and goes back to 1942 and 1943. In 1942, Yossarian is at a basic training camp at Lowry Field, in 1943 at the C Training Camp at Santa Ana California and finally arrives at Pianosa Italy in 1944.

The number of times Yossarian flies the different missions is also conveyed to the reader through a series of flashbacks. Chapter six takes the reader to the previous Fall when twenty-five flying missions were required and Yossarian reached twenty-three by flying six missions in six days. At this point

Colonel Cathcart became the new group commander and in celebration raised the number of missions to thirty. Once again Heller conveys to the reader Yossarian's desperate attempts to get off combat duty through a number of flashbacks. For instance, after leaving the hospital in chapter one, Yossarian unsuccessfully tries to persuade Doc Daneeka to help him and considers refusing to fly any more missions. However, when the doctor refuses to help him he appeals before Major Major and when he too rejects Yossarian's plea the bombardier visits Doc Daneeka once again in chapter seventeen. As all his attempts are thwarted he requests the Chaplain for help and the chaplain responds vigorously but without any solution. After Yossarian is wounded over Leghorn, the psychiatrist at the hospital certifies him insane but confuses him with another patient who gets sent home instead of Yossarian. Ultimately, in chapter thirty-eight Heller's hero refuses to enter into a pact with Cathcart and Korn and deserts. Information about other important events in the novel is provided to the reader through a number of flashbacks. For instance in chapter ten Yossarian decides not to fly the first Bologna mission and during another flashback in chapter twenty-four it is revealed that while on the Avignon mission Snowden died in Yossarian's arms smearing his uniform with blood. Thereafter Yossarian refused to wear any uniform as the sight of a military dress revoked the memories of Snowden's horrible death in his mind. A final flashback revealing the full import of Snowden's death occurs in chapter forty-one.

The technique of parody and Black Humour has been used in the novel in order to juxtapose the comic with the catastrophic and thereby heighten the terror of war. The author wanted his readers to laugh and then look back with horror at what they were laughing. Thus Heller parodies a situation like war and there is continuous play of humour and horror in the novel. Although there are several hilarious moments, the readers are not allowed to forget the terror of war. The four hundred odd pages of the novel are brilliant sketches in Black Humour where Yossarian consistently acts as the insane bombardier desperately trying to survive the stupidity of war. Louis Hasley believes that "the laughter repeatedly breaks through the tight net of frustration through which the characters struggle only to sink back as the net repairs itself and holds the readers imprisoned in its outrageous bonds" (Hasley, 190).

Critics including Brustein have described *Catch 22* as a 'very funny book' (Brustein, 44). But despite the laughter that the novel evokes, the overall impression is of horror rather than humour. The laughter evoked is not the kind that unites us warmly in sympathy with the human race as we enjoy its foibles, but rather reveals the bitter ironies of experience. Laughter is caused by incongruity, by a frustrating of our expectation and is cynical and frightening and although Heller seems to be trivializing war, he presents a dark vision of the world through a unique mixture of comedy and despair.

War is indeed presented as a black situation and in the novel riotous humour all of a sudden gives way to black tragedy and *vice-versa*. The big joke of the Catch itself is an instance of Black Humour and exemplifies this condition more than anything else. Yossarian wants to be grounded on the grounds of insanity but cannot because an insane person would never know the difference between sanity and insanity. Comic situations are interspersed with continuous intrusion of horror. An outright comic scene in the novel does evoke laughter but also evokes an uneasy feeling of morbidity. Repeated references to Yossarian sitting naked on a tree during Snowden's funeral evoke laughter, but when we read about Snowden's evisceration we are filled with horror. The soldier in white a war casualty who is described as being encased from head to toe in plastic initially evokes laughter, he even becomes a butt of ridicule for malingering soldiers who have become insensitive due to a continuous exposure to death and violence. However, a patient fully bandaged lying in a military hospital is a war reality that also sends shivers down one's spine. "The soldier in white was encased from head to toe in plaster and gauze. He had two useless legs and two useless arms" (*Catch 22*, 16).

The behaviour of the characters, their dialogues cause laughter but also present the doomed nature of the world. Much of the novel's comedy is generated by Yossarian's acrobatic maneuvers and insane tactics to keep himself alive, in accordance with his grimly accurate assessment that people in both armies are trying to kill him. But his futile and frustrating attempts to escape the chaos of the war, the clutches of the military bureaucracy and the monstrous principle of *Catch 22*, which has its stubborn grip on everybody's life, are frightening.

The novel had a profound impact on the reading public of the 1960s and 1970s. So much so that when Joseph Heller died in the year 1999, a naval officer, named James Webb wrote a commentary on the novel, paying a fervent tribute to Heller and *Catch 22* on the op-ed page of the *Wall Street Journal*. Webb was a graduate of the naval academy who had fought as a marine in the Vietnam War where he was wounded. After he returned from Vietnam he was honoured and later appointed secretary of the navy by President Ronald Reagan. With this background, Webb should have expressed reservations about a novel, which ridicules war and the military with such vehemence. However, Webb was all praise for it. He said in this article that *Catch 22's* lasting greatness was beyond dispute and was of the opinion that the novel's greatness lay in the truths, Heller revealed about the war especially his message that wars dehumanize, and few soldiers march happily towards battlefields. Webb especially praised *Catch 22* for having stripped away cant and hypocrisy and revealing how difficult it is to serve in the war. Webb was actually in Vietnam when he read the novel in 1969 and said, "from that lonely place of blood, and misery and disease...I found a soul mate who helped me face the next day and all the days and months that followed" (Webb, 1).

Despite an all-pervasive note of morbidity, gloom and despair *Catch 22* ends on a positive note. The protagonist Yossarian chooses the principle of beautiful, glorious life by fleeing to Sweden. Heller's message in the novel clearly seems to be that war must be avoided at all costs because it is ugly, causes widespread destruction and negates life.

Kurt Vonnegut: *Slaughterhouse Five*

6

American fiction of the 1960s and 70s was not only exciting and abundant but also innovative and unique as it underwent some fundamental transformation of style and value, built on a deep cultural change. In his oft quoted work *The Death of the Novel* Ronald Sukenick spelled out why conventional realistic and even modernistic fiction, narrative grounded in social manners, natural science, psychology and myth had become inadequate in the post-war world leaving intellectual writers with little hope beyond silence:

> "Fiction constitutes a way of looking at the world. Therefore I will begin by considering how the world looks in what I think we may begin to call the contemporary post-realistic novel. Realistic fiction presupposed chronological time as the medium of a plotted narrative, an irreducible individual psyche as the subject of its characterization, and, above all, the ultimate concrete reality of things as the object and rationale of its description. In the world of post-realism, however, all of these absolutes have become absolutely problematic." (Lundquist, 71)

Sukenick was of the view that reality is simply our experience, and objectivity is, of course, an illusion and literature does not exist. Reading and writing are merely "things to do like eating and drinking and making love, ways of maintaining a considered boredom in the face of the abyss" (Lundquist, 70). Therefore Sukenick called for a 're-invention' in fiction and Kurt Vonnegut's novel *Slaughterhouse Five* published in 1969 can be cited as an example of the type of re-invention that Sukenick called for in postmodernist fiction. The novel abandoned the traditional structure of linear time and solidly fixable space and used the device of fantasy and science fiction to underscore its main theme, the insanity of war and the dilemma of modern Man caught in its absurdity. In the novel the readers are introduced to aliens called Tralfamadorians who abduct the protagonist Billy Pilgrim in a flying saucer and take him to planet Tralfamadore. After that, Billy continuously escapes from earth into an extraterrestrial world in order to escape the atrocities such as war, death and destruction perpetuated by 'Earthlings'.

In keeping with the postmodernist tradition *Slaughterhouse Five* can be regarded as an example of metafiction, which attempts to pose questions about the relationship between fiction and reality. In her work *Metafiction: The Theory and Practice of Self-Conscious Fiction,* Patricia Waugh defines metafiction as "fictional writing which self-consciously and systematically draws attention to its status as an artifact in order to pose questions about the relationship between fiction and reality.... Metafiction explores a theory of writing fiction through the practice of writing fiction" (Waugh, 1). Postmodernist theorist William Gass coined the term 'metafiction' in 1970. Commenting on American fiction of the 1960s, Gass pointed out that a new term was needed for the emerging genre of experimental texts that openly broke with the tradition of literary realism dominant in American literature. The term was used to describe the works of writers like John Barth, Donald Barthleme, Raymond Federman and Robert Coover because not only did these writers violate or subvert the dominant conventions of novel writing but also explicitly discussed the act of experimentation while they performed this very act. Metafiction is therefore fiction that self-consciously reflects upon its own nature, its modes of production and its intended effect on the reader. In consonance with the strategies employed by the writers of metafiction, Vonnegut continuously raises questions about reality and fiction in the novel. For instance, a large section is centred on the debate whether fiction can effectively portray a massacre as terrible as Dresden and a situation as absurd as war. Simultaneously the author realizes that 'realistic' fiction would not be able to depict the trauma and violence of battle because one more account of the horrors of war with realistic details and statistics would be unable to articulate a personal sense of shock to a public inundated with daily reports of violent death. Therefore Vonnegut dispenses with reality and employs a number of metafictive devices like violation of narrative levels and reliance on unconventional and experimental techniques in order to reveal his anguish.

Linda Hutcheon calls *Slaughterhouse Five* an example of 'historiographic metafiction' because it echoes texts and contexts of the past and displays great 'intertextuality'. Hutcheon is of the view that 'historiographic metafiction' works to 'situate itself within historical discourse without surrendering its autonomy as fiction'. She argues that the novel is based on a historical event and 'counterpointed to this historical context' is Billy Pilgrim whose fantasy life acts as an allegory of the author's own displacements and postponement, his numerous other novels that prevented him from writing his Dresden novel. The texts and contexts, 'intertextuality' is seen in the creation of planet Tralfamadore which is from the author's *The Sirens of Titans*, Billy's home in Ilium is from *Player Piano* while characters from *Mother Night* and *God Bless You, Mr. Rosewater* also make an appearance in *Slaughterhouse Five*. There is another kind of 'intertextuality' displayed in the novel as well. Hutcheon opines that there are allusions to Herman Hesse's *Journey to the East* and to various works of science fiction. Popular and high-art intertexts mingle: *Valley of Dolls* blends with the poems of William Blake and Theodore Roethke and finally there are real historical intertexts like documentaries on Dresden which mingle with the historical fiction of Stephen Crane and Louis Ferdinand Celine. The self-reflexivity and intertextuality makes the novel extremely interesting.

The author's horror and dislike of war is a theme, which is directly or indirectly present in all his novels and this is because of his having participated in the Second Great War as a soldier who was a witness to senseless killing and violence. In the modern world, war has become a technological horror with the threat of nuclear Holocaust looming large. In all his writings

Vonnegut displays a suspicion towards science and technology and expresses a fear that Man's obsession with nuclear weapons may lead to the outbreak of yet another war. Further through his anti-war statements, he seems to convey the idea that 'righteousness' can never be a cause for fighting any war. Americans ostensibly fought the Second World War so that 'right', that is freedom and democracy could prevail over 'wrong' that is totalitarianism and fascism. The author strongly debunks this idea for no cause can justify a life-threatening situation such as war. Although *Slaughterhouse Five* is about World War II, Vonnegut like Mailer and Heller makes a scathing attack on America's obsession with fighting wars. When the novel was published American soldiers were fighting a fierce battle in the jungles of Vietnam and many historians believe that the Vietnam War was unnecessary and was the outcome of America's desire to control the destiny of South East Asia. Through his antiwar statements Kurt Vonnegut manages to establish an essential and unusual bond between himself and his readers. Although he has no political ideologies to discuss, the author has conveyed the idea to the readers of the futility of war (no matter what the causes are) and also the idea of human vulnerability in the face of war. Critics are of the opinion that despite all the complexities of style and technique the author is essentially a pacifist and a champion of humane values.

There is a strong autobiographical element in *Slaughterhouse Five*. Vonnegut had participated in the Second World War and suffered tremendously as a Prisoner of War (POW). He was taken prisoner by the Germans during the Battle of Bulge and survived the Allied firebombing of Dresden inside the cellar of a slaughterhouse. The bombing of Dresden had a profound impact on Vonnegut and his views on war, death, technology and human nature were all affected by this experience. David Goldsmith is of the opinion that rarely has a single incident so dominated the work of a writer (Goldsmith, 40). In this respect Vonnegut is similar to Ernest Hemingway whose participation in World War I proved to be crucial to all his writing. The wound acquired by Hemingway as an ambulance driver from a trench mortar shell played a very important role in his artistic development. The wound affected him not only physically but also psychologically. In all his fiction as it is well-known, the Hemingway hero is a wounded man, be it Frederic Henry of *A Farewell to Arms* or Jake Barnes of *The Sun also Rises* or Robert Jordan of *For Whom the Bell Tolls*. Vonnegut too seems to be psychologically influenced by war as is seen in most of his major fiction although *Slaughterhouse Five* is his only war novel. Yet the novels, which do not treat war as the primary subject, nevertheless comment on its effects and in an oblique way the protagonists look for meaning in a war ravaged world.

In novels like *The Sirens of Titans* Vonnegut satirizes the Martians and their military regimentation as they plan their unsuccessful attack on Earth. In *God Bless You, Mr Rosewater*, the character Eliot Rosewater suffers from the memory of a World War II episode during which he had mistakenly killed a German boy and this episode is responsible for his mental collapse while in *Jailbird* the protagonist is haunted by the memories of war. In *Deadeye Dick*, Vonnegut even refers to World War III. But in all these novels the humorous antics of the various characters and the device of science fiction ease the shock that the descriptions of war produce. Although Vonnegut's Dresden experiences are mentioned in an introduction he wrote for the 1966 reissue of *Mother Night*, the historical facts are not developed in the novel itself and the author only briefly describes the firebombing of Dresden in the above novel. In *Mother Night* Adolf Eichmann whose character is based on a historical figure, is portrayed as a crazed clown. Laughing at war is a kind of protective measure in this novel for it shields us from the horrifying specter of Eichmann's six million murders, and seems to be the only sane response to the insanity of war. Significantly, *Slaughterhouse Five* although funny is not as wildly humorous as the writer's previous writing. The lack of outrageous comedy is not a flaw but rather a comment upon how deeply Vonnegut feels about the bombing of Dresden. The novel though funny in parts has a somber tone and the humour used by Vonnegut can be termed as 'gallows humour'. The novel is based not on imagination but on a real historical episode, a Holocaust that Vonnegut suffered and lived to write about. Although in the novel the author laughs at war, he also emphasizes the fact that there is absolutely nothing comical or funny about it and uses humour as a device to cope with the absurdity of the human situation in the face of war.

Kurt Vonnegut 'brooded' about the Dresden atrocity for twenty-three years. He wanted to write a novel about it, but could not bring himself to do so as he was unable to purge the intense pain and anguish which were bottled up inside him. Thus, for twenty-three long years there was no Catharsis for Vonnegut. The author believes that he could not write the novel and face his past because no words could describe a massacre as horrible as Dresden. The subtitle of the novel is 'The Children's Crusade and a Duty Dance with Death'. The author laments that our lives have indeed become a dance with death, death seems to have become a trivial issue in modern times confronting us at every step. Vonnegut emphasizes the triviality of death by using an inane expression 'so it goes' every time he refers to it.

The Dresden massacre caused the death of nearly 135,000 civilians. Owing to the ingenuity of modern technology, an entire city was turned into a mass grave. What made the bombing even more terrible for Vonnegut was that it was carried out by people from his own country; by the British and American air force, and that while so many people were killed by his own countrymen, he remained unscathed, and alive, protected as he was by the shelter of an airtight slaughterhouse during the raid. As planes from his country bombed Dresden, Vonnegut felt that he was also responsible for the mass destruction carried out by the Allied forces. For twenty-three years therefore, Vonnegut was torn between a desire to forget Dresden, and a passion to reproduce what he saw there. In the opening chapter Vonnegut describes his attempts at writing the story of Dresden:

> "I would hate to tell you what this lousy little book cost me in money and anxiety and time. When I got home from the Second World War twenty-three years ago, I thought it would be easy for me to write about the destruction of Dresden, since all I would have to do

> would be to report what I had seen. And I thought, too, that it would be a masterpiece or at least make me a lot of money, since the subject was so big. But not many words about Dresden came from my mind then...not enough of them to make a book anyway. And not many words come now, either." (*SHV*, 4)

The guilt of survival inhibited Vonnegut from writing about the massacre and liberating himself from the trauma that remained deeply etched in his mind for two long decades. This phenomenon called 'guilt of survival' is closely associated with victims who have survived mass atrocities. Robert Jay Lifton a psychoanalyst, writing about this phenomenon comments on the "increasing gap that human beings face between their technological capacity for perpetrating atrocities and the imaginative ability to confront their full actuality" (Greiner, 43). Further, victims who suffer atrocities like bombing raids experience what Lifton calls 'psychic numbing', realizing the full implication of their suffering many years or perhaps months later. Sometimes when the victims look back at their trauma, they feel guilty about having come out of the atrocity unscathed while some of their fellow sufferers have succumbed to death, insanity or other kinds of mishaps. The guilt then tortures these victims in addition to the memories of the atrocity.

Having had a close interaction with victims of the Hiroshima raid Lifton is of the opinion that this encounter changed his feelings about his own (Lifton's) death as well as about collective deaths. For the first time he realized that suspicions of Apocalypse could no longer be laughed away as a delusion of the world coming to an end. The survivors of the Hiroshima atrocity experienced a sense of 'dislocation', 'absurdity' and guilt, which 'destroyed their previous assumptions of a rational universe'. Donald J. Greiner feels that Lifton's analysis of atrocity is particularly relevant to Vonnegut's novel:

> "By writing *Slaughterhouse Five*, Vonnegut narrows the gap between his realization of the technological capacity for total destruction and his ability to confront barbarity because the book is a fictionalized account of an atrocity personally experienced. Surviving the

annihilation of 135,000 civilians not only sharpened Vonnegut's awareness of his own death but also brought home his relationship to collective death on a nearly unimaginable scale." (Greiner, 45)

One of Lifton's conclusions is especially relevant in this case: "Survivors felt guilty about remaining alive while others died, and also experienced an amorphous sense of having been a part of, having imbibed the overall evil of the atrocity" (Greiner, 50). Greiner further believes that while no one can speak for Vonnegut's private reactions his novel suggests that Billy Pilgrim suffers the same sense of guilt by virtue of his unusual status during the Dresden raid. He is as was Vonnegut, an American who survived the destruction of the city of Dresden by British and American forces. Billy shares the guilt of both the Allied victimizers who slaughtered and the American victims who survived. His trips to Tralfamadore suggest the kind of psychic numbing, which Lifton discusses. Vonnegut must have experienced the same sort of 'double guilt', and the guilt may have inhibited for years, his efforts to write *Slaughterhouse Five* his 'famous book about Dresden'. If Billy is regarded as a partial mask for the author, then his psychological condition would be similar to that of Vonnegut. The writing of the novel therefore has most likely been a liberating process for the author and by finally completing his novel about Dresden, Vonnegut was able to purge himself of guilt, which made him silent for twenty-three years.

Vonnegut's novel unlike that of Mailer's and Heller's is based on two major events in the history of the Second World War. The first one was the Battle of Bulge, which was also known as the Ardennes Offensive, the last major German Offensive on the Western front, and the other was the Allied firebombing of Dresden. During this battle, most of which was fought in the mountainous Ardennes Forest in Luxembourg many American troops were taken Prisoners of War (POWs), it is this battle that has been mentioned in the novel and it is during this that the German forces capture Billy Pilgrim and his friend Roland Weary. Vonnegut describes the Battle of Bulge as a mopping up operation by the German army.

The Allied firebombing of Dresden was a controversial action, which was kept hidden from the world for many years. The author informs his readers that when he finally decided to write his famous war novel and approached the authorities for information he was denied access to the 'top secret':

> "I wrote the Air Force back then, asking for details about the raid on Dresden, who ordered it, how many planes did it, why they did it.... I was answered by a man who like myself was in public relations. He said that he was sorry, but the information was top secret still. I read the letter out loud to my wife and I said '*secret my god from who?*'" (*SHV*, 10)

Dresden was the capital of the German state of Saxony and was firebombed by the Allied Air Force, primarily the British Royal Air Force and the United States Army Air Force (USAF) over three days from February, 13-15 towards the end of the war in 1945. Those who carried out the massacre were never held accountable for war crimes and the breach of the Geneva Convention. Dresden was considered a city of little war related, industrial or strategic importance and thus was considered a safe city which would never be bombed. An American POW in the novel writes as much to his wife: "Dear Margaret, we are leaving for Dresden today. Don't worry it will never be bombed" (*SHV*, 128). However, Dresden was bombed. It is believed that the bombing was carried out at the request of Russia in order to attack a German armoured division in transit through the city. It is also believed that Churchill ordered the bombing because he wanted to impress the Russians with Allied air power. The Red Army was advancing rapidly from the East in order to occupy Germany and Churchill feared being forced into an inferior position at the Yalta talks. Ironically, the Yalta meetings ended before the Dresden raid.

Vonnegut adheres to historical authenticity of the Dresden attack by citing passages from David Irving's book *The Destruction of Dresden* particularly quotations from the introduction by Ira C. Eaker, a retired officer of the United States Air Force (USAF) and from the foreword by the British Air Marshal Robert Saundby. In the novel, as Billy recovers at a hospital from an airplane crash, he finds himself in a semi-private room with a Harvard history professor named Rumfoord, who is documenting a history of the U.S. Army Air Corps in World War II. Rumfoord needs to review the key historical texts about the war's major bombings and air battles and he is in possession of certain texts and documents that justify bombardment of civilian targets. Rumfoord is also in possession of David Irving's book and Vonnegut quotes the two prefaces of Irving's book in his novel. The bombing of Dresden is justified in Eaker's foreword, and this is quoted in the novel:

> "I deeply regret that British and U.S. bombers killed 135,000 people in the attack on Dresden, but I remember who started the last war and I regret even more the loss of more than 5,000,000 Allied lives in the necessary effort to completely defeat and utterly destroy Nazism." (*SHV*, 161)

Vonnegut ridicules General Eaker's reasoning with minimal indirect commentary, not because he tries to excuse Dresden but because he assumes that to balance an Allied atrocity with a German one is to neutralize and thus to expiate guilt. Greiner is of the view that for Eaker guilt belonged nowhere since both the sides indulged in several atrocities, but for Vonnegut the guilt is universal. Another text, which is in Rumfoord's possession, is the speech of President Harry Truman, announcing the bombing of Hiroshima and Nagasaki. President Truman's speech justifies the terrible bombing of these cities and is quoted in Vonnegut's novel: "We are now prepared to obliterate more rapidly and completely every productive enterprise the Japanese have above ground in any city...we shall completely destroy Japan's power to make war" (*SHV*, 161). All the texts which are in Rumfoord's possession justify mass bombardment of civilian populations, a theory of war developed as early as 1920s by the Italian military theorist General Givolio Douket and the American aviator General Billy Mitchell.

Vonnegut informs his readers that the city of Dresden was immensely beautiful and extremely vulnerable when it was bombed. When the raid was carried out in February 1945, it was virtually undefended, bursting with hundreds of thousands of refugees from the East and a total of 26,000 prisoners. In October 1944, Dresden's anti-aircraft guns were dismantled and once this happened the civilian population started believing that the city would never be attacked. Irving says in his book that only papier-mâché dummies remained on the hills outside to defend the city once the guns were dismantled.

Billy's description of Dresden burning is similar to historical accounts. The description of charred bodies, bodies of mere schoolgirls who were boiled alive in a water tower by his own countrymen is verified by Irving's book. Most of the victims died due to suffocation and the novel gives an account of how the entire city turned into a mass grave. The dead bodies were stacked before the mass cremations—first layer with heads pointed left and second layer with feet pointed left. Perhaps the novel's, two most shocking events with historical validity are the Americans strafing the city even after most people had died during the bombing and the execution of Edgar Derby (Billy Pilgrim's fellow POW) for taking a teapot. The strafing incident, although minor when compared to the tons of firebombs dropped, illustrates the Allied policy of total destruction and underscores the senselessness of the atrocity. Vonnegut says in the novel: "Absolutely everybody in the city was supposed to be dead, regardless of what they were, and that anybody that moved in it represented a flaw in the design. There were to be no moon men at all" (*SHV*, 155).

The idea of strafing the surviving civilians he tells us was to 'hasten the end of the war'. The irony of Derby's execution after the raid is supported by Irving's account of American and French-Canadian prisoners being shot for taking food from wrecked shops. This is an instance of the warped sense of justice prevailing in a world, which could perpetuate an unethical act like the Dresden horror and yet meticulously observe the letter of the law as it applies to petty looting. To make sure that the readers get his point, Vonnegut tells us that Derby's execution is the novel's climax:

> "I think the climax of the book will be the execution of poor old Edgar Derby...the irony is so great. A whole city gets burned down and thousands and thousands of

> people are killed and then this one American foot soldier is arrested in the ruins for taking a teapot. And he's given a regular trial and then he's shot by firing squad." (*SHV*, 4)

The beautiful city of Dresden is reduced to rubble after the firebombing. When Billy had arrived in the city it had appeared as enchanting and beautiful like the picture of heaven, but his description of the firebombing of Dresden approximates the picture of Hell with its purgatorial fires.

There is no conventional story line in the novel and the action moves back and forth in time. This is because its protagonist Billy Pilgrim continuously travels between periods of his life oscillating between the past, present and future. This time tripping technique used in the novel will be discussed later in the chapter. Though the novel is based on Vonnegut's personal account of the Dresden massacre, and the protagonist and the author share a common experience, Vonnegut as author maintains a certain distance from the second chapter onwards. Billy's story is not exactly similar to that of the author's because aliens supposedly abduct Billy and later he travels to their planet time and again to flee the insanity of the world. Whether this is really true or a flight of Billy's imagination is left for the reader to decide. In the opening chapter, Vonnegut describes his efforts to gather information about the firebombing of Dresden from a 'war buddy' who shared the experience with him, and after having obtained the desired information he promises his friend's wife that the book would not be just another war novel with potential roles for John Wayne and Frank Sinatra. By subtitling his novel 'The Children's Crusade' Vonnegut relates all modern warfare to the original Children's Crusade of 1212 A.D. when 30,000 children volunteered to go to Palestine, but half of them drowned in ship wrecks while the remaining half were sold as slaves in North Africa.

There were approximately seven Crusades between the years 1095 and 1271. The Christian powers of Europe sent these military expeditions to Palestine in a mostly unsuccessful attempt to regain the possession of the Holy Land from the Muslims.

The Children's Crusade supposedly took place after the Fourth Crusade when a boy named Stephen Cloyens began preaching in France claiming that Jesus had visited him and told him to lead the next Crusade. His preaching gained him a considerable following and as many as 30,000 children decided to go to the Holy Land. However, owing to the long distance many of them died on the journey while others were abducted and taken to Tunisia where they were sold as slaves.

In the second chapter, Vonnegut focuses on Billy Pilgrim who like the author himself was born in Ilium in 1922 and grew up there too. A funny-looking, weak youth he does reasonably well in high school, enrolled in the night classes at the Ilium School of optometry and is drafted into the army during World War II. He trains as a Chaplain's assistant in South Carolina where an umpire officiates during practice battles and announces who survives and who dies before they all sit down to lunch together. Billy's father dies in a hunting accident shortly before he ships overseas to join an infantry regiment in Luxembourg. He is thrown into the Battle of Bulge in Belgium and is almost immediately taken prisoner behind German lines. Just before his capture, he experiences his first incident of time shifting: he sees the entirety of his life, from beginning to the end, in one sweep, what Vonnegut calls coming 'Unstuck in time'. As a POW, Billy is transported in a crowded railway boxcar to a camp in Germany. As the train journey begins, Billy's fellow prisoner and comrade, Roland Weary dies of gangrene resulting from his injured foot. He blames Pilgrim for his plight, and a paranoid little soldier named Paul Lazzaro swears to avenge him by having Billy killed. Eventually the dilapidated prisoners are unloaded at a camp for Russain POWs where they are deloused, showered, given overcoats and marched into a compound for British officers who have been captured earlier in the war. The British POWs are organized, clean, healthy and disciplined and organize a welcome dinner and a pantomime for the new arrivals. Billy suffers a breakdown and gets a shot of morphine that sends him time tripping again. Within a few days the Americans march into the beautiful city of Dresden to begin work, mainly bottling a honey like Vitamin supplement for pregnant women. They are housed in a slaughterhouse bearing the number five. At one point, they are urged to join the 'Free America Corps' to fight the Russians by Howard Campbell, an American Nazi propagandist who urges the Americans to fight the Russians and promises them food and repatriation in return.

One night the city is firebombed while Billy and his fellow prisoners and four guards take shelter in an airtight meat locker. When they emerge from their shelter the ruins of Dresden look like the face of the moon. For a few days the Americans are forced to excavate corpses from the rubble and several days later when the Russian forces capture the city Billy's involvement in the war ends. Billy returns to Illium finishes optometry school and gets engaged to Valencia Merble the obese daughter of the school founder. After the engagement he suffers a nervous breakdown, and is admitted to a veteran's hospital where he is given shock treatment. It is at this hospital that he meets Professor Rumfoord the History Professor. Billy recuperates, marries Valencia Merble has two children and as time passes acquires the 'trappings of the suburban American dream': a Cadillac, a stately home with modern appliances, a bejeweled wife and the presidency of the Lion's Club. He is not aware of keeping any secrets from himself but at his 18th wedding anniversary party upon hearing the barbershop quartet Billy breaks down because it triggers off the memory of Dresden.

The night after his daughter's wedding in 1967 as he later reveals on a radio talk show, two feet high aliens called Tralfamadorians abduct Billy and take him in their flying saucer to planet Tralfamadore where they mate him with a movie actress Montana Wildhack. She like Billy has been brought from Earth to live under a transparent geodesic dome in a zoo where the aliens observe 'extraterrestrial' curiosities. The Tralfamadorians explain to Billy their perception of time and how its entire sweep exists for them simultaneously in the fourth dimension. Tralfamadorians prefer to look at life's nicer moments and with their cosmic vision are puzzled by Billy's concern about finding a cure for wars that plague the Earth. When he returns to Earth, Billy initially says nothing of his experiences. In 1968, he boards a chartered plane to go to an optometry conference in Montreal but the plane crashes and Billy the only survivor is taken to a hospital where a brain surgeon operates upon him. While on her way to visit Billy at the hospital Valencia dies of carbon monoxide poisoning after her car meets with an accident. When Billy is discharged from the hospital, he feels that the time is ripe to tell the world what he has learnt from the Tralfamadorians. He also makes a tape recording of the account of his death which he predicts will occur in 1976 after Chicago has been hydrogen-bombed by the Chinese. Looking into the future Billy insists that he has seen the moment of his death several times declaring that a vengeful man named Paul Lazzaro will hire someone to shoot him. The novel ends with Billy travelling to Dresden once more and describing the end of the war on a beautiful spring morning. Ironically, spring signifies rejuvenation and rebirth but everything in Dresden is dead, burnt, reduced to ashes.

The protagonist of the novel has been scarred by the war, which has left an indelible mark on his psyche. Throughout the novel Pilgrim exhibits signs of what psychoanalysts call post-traumatic stress disorder. Psychoanalysts believe that after an intensely harrowing situation like combat, extreme stress can disrupt normal functioning of the brain with symptoms like hallucinations, hysteria and even insanity. Billy displays all these symptoms as he is overcome by uncontrollable bouts of weeping, suffers from insomnia and even appears insane when he repeatedly refers to his abduction by the aliens. He frequently oscillates between the past and the present, claiming that he is a witness to his own death. A possible explanation for Billy's frequent travelling into time can be his fractured state of mind and his anguished soul, which is unable to forget the Dresden Holocaust. The readers are also made aware of the fact that Billy suffered a mental breakdown and received treatment at an asylum.

Such intense suffering can dehumanize the individual and the author emphasizes this idea through a number of images that completely depersonalize his characters. For instance he does not refer to the characters as prisoners or Americans; he simply calls them human beings. Thereafter he depersonalizes them even further as they are no longer individuals but "a warm, squirming, sighing earth on the floor of the boxcar" (*SHV*, 62). Such images continue when the prisoners are referred to as a 'liquid' that the guards must coax into flowing out of the boxcars once they reach the prison camp. Edgar Derby and Paul Lazzaro make their appearance at this point in the novel and are impersonally introduced as the 'best and worst bodies'. The author admits that there are no characters in this story because as a consequence of war they have become 'sick, listless playthings of enormous forces' and are manipulated by circumstances and forces in ways, which limit their freedom for character defining actions.

Much of the cast in the novel make only brief appearances which may cause striking impressions but do not lead to any in-depth analysis or detailed characterization. Hence Vonnegut briefly mentions soldiers like Wild Bob and Roland Weary but does not develop their character.

Thus despite being the protagonist of the novel, Billy Pilgrim's characterization is also limited and he is sick and listless and as his name suggests becomes a contemporary Pilgrim progressing through an absurd world. Billy has absolutely no clue about how to face the world, which is being ravaged by war. Unassertive and indecisive "Billy functions like a Charlie Chaplain character let off in a world of pain and suffering" (Dhar, 40). He is unbelievably passive is pushed, prodded, bullied, beaten and threatened and yet he does not react. A critic Peter J. Reed looks upon him as a child duped into the Children's Crusade. Billy is required to fulfill many roles in the novel; that of a businessman, polished convention speaker, participant in talk shows, a devastated POW and a shattered soldier, but he is never convincing and does not develop as a character during the course of the novel. He is a mere puppet in the hands of forces which control him and since he is devastated by the war he loses the will to live and gets 'unstuck in time', travelling continuously between the past and the present.

The phenomenon of death further obliterates the identity of the individual and comes as a final blow to human beings dehumanized by war. Vonnegut upholds the principle of life in *Slaughterhouse Five* and assails a life-negating situation like war, which causes innumerable deaths. Broer is of the opinion that innumerable deaths occur in the novel: "If one counts deaths that are predicted or imagined as well as those that occur, there may be a greater proliferation of corpses in *Slaughterhouse Five* than in any other twentieth century novel" (Broer, 90).

A number of deaths are caused by factors like starvation, incineration, torture, hanging, poisoning, bombing, gassing and shooting. Soldiers, priests, officers, Robert Kennedy and Martin Luther King, Pilgrim's mother, father and wife all die. Vonnegut even mentions the death of Jesus Christ. In the novel everything or everybody dies, entire towns, cities and ever the universe gets wiped out. Many deaths in the novel are ironic, especially that of the unfortunate school teacher Edgar Derby who survives the battle of Bulge only to be shot for plundering a teapot from the ruins of the blazing city.

Vonnegut also offers another view of death when he describes the Tralfamadorian view that all moments always have and always will exist and that death is just one moment in anyone's life. The Tralfamadorians enjoy the good moments and ignore the bad ones but the author does not accept this solution because he believes that fighting and death caused by meaningless warfare have to come to an end. He finally comes to the conclusion that suffering and death is caused as a result of their own murderousness for men derive immense pleasure from the inhuman actions involving torture and destruction of their fellows.

The subtitle of the novel is 'The Children's Crusade' and Vonnegut draws a parallel between the Children's Crusade of Medieval times and modern warfare. The senselessness of this historical Crusade provides the author with a parallel to the destruction of Dresden which too was pointless. The starting point of the comparison begins when Vonnegut's friend's wife Mary O' Hare insists that men like to think of war as a 'manly pursuit' whereas it is a childish venture fought by babies:

> "Then she turned to me let me see how angry she was and that the anger was for me. She had been talking to herself, so what she said was a fragment of a much larger conversation, 'You were just babies then', she said '...I nodded that this was true. We had been foolish virgins in the war, right at the end of childhood'." (*SHV*, 12-13)

Vonnegut agrees with Mary and promises to call the novel 'The Children's Crusade'. Peter J. Reed expresses the view that the obvious parallels between the Children's Crusade and the soldiers fighting in the army are that the people sent to die in both cases were young, innocent, and victims of circumstances they were unable to comprehend. The army is composed of young soldiers, nearly children who find themselves hapless pawns of forces they cannot overcome. The soldiers of Billy Pilgrim's captive regiment are also extremely young, boys in their teens. The Colonel, who commands the British prisoners in the POW camp where the captive soldiers are ultimately lodged, had always imagined that the war was being fought by men. When he sees the Americans shaved and cleaned he realizes for the first time how young they are and is shocked: "My god—It's the Children's Crusade" (*SHV*, 91).

Billy Pilgrim, young, gawky and childishly perplexed is also like a crusader who starts out on a holy mission as the chaplain's assistant. He appears to be childlike-naïve, innocent and passive. He is the perfect representational figure for the conception of war being a Children's Crusade.

In consonance with this aspect of war the entertainment the English POWs provide for the Americans is a modified children's pantomime, Cinderella. Reed makes another observation: "when the clean, healthy British POWs recoil from the unkempt, American POWs they divide the camp compound by the old childhood technique of scraping a groove in the ground with the heel" (Reed, 180). The Children's Crusade is thus a metaphor for all wars because the soldiers fighting the war seem to be like children involved (much against their will) in an adult quarrel. In addition, men maimed and dazed by the destruction of war are driven back into themselves in regressive ways and become childlike. Vonnegut depicts war as a terrifying unleashing of monstrous forces, which sweeps up the innocent children of men, dehumanizing and destroying them.

In many nineteenth century American novels war was portrayed as heroic and glorious. In the novel Mary O' Hare expresses a fear that like the traditional war novelists Vonnegut too would write a novel that would glorify war and this novel would subsequently be made into a film with actors like John Wayne and Frank Sinatra playing the role of brave, heroic warriors. Vonnegut however, assures Mary that his novel would never glorify combat. The Bible in his motel room tells him that the Lord destroyed Sodom and Gomorrah (because Sodomy was being practiced in these cities) using fire and brimstone, Lot and his family were spared because they were the children of God. Lot's wife was asked not to look back but touched by compassion she looked back at the smouldering city and turned into a pillar of salt. Vonnegut too looks back at Dresden like Lot's wife with sympathy and compassion not to exalt it but rather to debunk it.

The British POWs come under a scathing attack as these soldiers idealize and elevate war. In Vonnegut's novel the British POWs live in a self-supervised camp, they are clean, disciplined, immaculate and well stocked with goods. They exercise regularly, keep themselves well bathed and groomed and manage to preserve an atmosphere of sanity amidst the insanity of war. They have a relatively comfortable life compared to American POWs. It is not surprising therefore that the German commander in charge of the camp adores them because: "They were exactly what Englishmen ought to be. They made war look stylish and reasonable, and fun" (*SHV*, 81). The British prisoners are a model of conduct, transforming the ugly, horrifying realities of war into something beautiful and magical.

The American POWs on the other hand offer a great contrast to these 'stylish' men. They are filthy and bedraggled, and are described as "Starving, dirty, unshaven, staggering on their feet from exhaustion." Even Billy Pilgrim, the protagonist of the novel is not a typical war hero. He is described as 'farcical' and 'scrawny' and in chapter six Vonnegut describes him as a clown "arrayed in fur satin coat". There is nothing stylish about Billy's appearance and on the contrary he seems to be grotesque: "Billy was preposterous—six feet and three inches tall, with a chest and shoulders like a box of kitchen matches.... He didn't look like a soldier at all. He looked like a filthy flamingo" (*SHV*, 28-29).

Through the unkempt American POWs and the character of Pilgrim, Vonnegut wants to emphasize the fact that war is not stylish and magnificent but sordid and ugly and soldiers are not immaculate and handsome but disheveled and battered. Furthermore, the British soldiers are blissfully ignorant about the distasteful realities of war; they are living in great comfort due to a clerical error and the fancy scented soap and candles used by them were made from the fat of Jews, Gypsies, Fairies, Communists and other enemies of the Third Reich.

The British prisoners and their romantic ideals about the war are exposed when Billy goes to ease himself at midnight after the feast provided by them to their American counterparts. He finds his entire fellow Americans terribly sick with diarrhoea. Thus, sickness and suffering are the byproducts of war and heroism and romance have no place in it. By satirizing the British POWs the author shatters 'the ideal soldier myth'.

In the contemporary world, technology has become a bane for our society with countries amassing stockpiles of nuclear weapons. Vonnegut expresses skepticism about technological advancement that has led to an arms race, making the world an extremely dangerous place. When he describes the destruction of Dresden caused by modern technology he is at a loss for words as no analogy on Earth can depict the devastation: "Dresden was like the moon now, nothing but minerals. The stones were hot. Everybody else in the neighbourhood was dead" (*SHV*, 153). In the novel, the Tralfamadorians pose a great threat to the universe because they are experimenting with a new fuel and this experiment may blow up the entire universe. The fact that the end of the universe could be so sudden and so quick is indeed a frightening thought. Though Vonnegut writes about the Second World War, the novel is really about the next war and the continuous wars that human beings wage against each other and finally a war, which will be without limits and without meaning, a war that will end only when no one is left alive to fight it. The scenario seems bleak and depressing and through his novel Vonnegut warns us against this end of the world. John Culmer observes that in *Slaughterhouse Five*: "If the area of war is smaller than in *Catch 22*, the perspective of destruction is wider. It encompasses the destruction of the universe itself" (Culmer, 207).

In the modern world where the sanctity of human life is violated and where human beings have discarded principles like love, kindness, forgiveness and sympathy, moral degeneration takes place and even though war is destructive, human beings show great interest in it. To begin with, Vonnegut dismisses the idea that the bombing of Dresden could be justified on moral grounds. The moral context for the depiction of the Dresden raid is set up in the first chapter itself. As has been mentioned Vonnegut in his motel room reads about the destruction of Sodom and Gomorrah. Like the people of these cities the residents of Dresden were 'judged evil' and 'ripe for annihilation', by those who were 'good' and who were determined to banish fascism from this world. Hence the innocent citizens of Dresden were victimized and they died because they were nationals of, an 'evil' nation. The individual stories in the novel like those of Paul Lazzaro, Edgar Derby and Wild Bob also highlight the moral bankruptcy of human beings in the modern world. Through the character of Edgar Derby, who is arrested and shot by the Americans for plundering, Vonnegut tries to convey the idea that man irrespective of nationality or creed has the seeds of destruction in him. The forty-four-year old Derby is an intelligent, educated and a compassionate person (he cradled the dying Roland Weary in his arms) and his execution shocks the reader. Through the character of Wild Bob it is depicted that military men responsible for mass slaughter are morally degraded. Wild Bob selfishly leads his entire regiment to disaster, killing several human beings in the process. Paul Lazzaro (who vows to kill Billy) shows great insensitivity by robbing homes that have turned into rubble and amasses a huge fortune of diamonds, rubies and emeralds from the cellars of razed buildings.

As a part of the metafictive device *Slaughterhouse Five* dispenses with a traditional plot and structure and its construction is loose and episodic in keeping with the chaos and meaninglessness of war. The novel acquires a complicated structure owing to Vonnegut's essential 'aesthetic problem', which is how to describe a reality that is beyond human imagination. The author confiding in the reader reveals the awesome difficulty he faced while attempting to construct his story in a chronological order. When he failed, he endeavoured to 'outline' his story in the opening chapter of the novel by illustrating it on wallpaper with his daughter's crayons. Peter J. Reed explaining the diagram constructed by the author writes: "At the center of Vonnegut's material in the wallpaper outline cross-hatched across the sheet is the Dresden raid. From that central event he extends a web outward in time and space" (Reed, 180). Despite the fact that Dresden was the central point of his story, he was unable to outline his tale in a sequential manner.

Vonnegut sets up a frame for the story with a preface in the first chapter. This is yet another strategy used by writers of metafiction. Therefore, the first chapter is not about Billy Pilgrim, but a preamble about how the author came to write the story. Vonnegut apologizes about the fact that the novel is so 'short and jumbled and jangled' and explains that this is because there is nothing 'intelligent to say about a massacre'. In the opening chapter itself the author plays with fantasy and reality claiming 'all this happened, more or less' and when writing about Pilgrim's war experience he often appears himself though briefly followed by the narrator's note 'That was I. That was me. That was the author of this book.'

Slaughterhouse Five is structured like the Tralfamadorian novel. The aliens who abduct Billy tell him about their novels as he is being transported towards their planet. His captors offer him the only book in English that they have Jacqueline Susan's *Valley of Dolls*, which is to be placed in a museum. The aliens allow Billy to look at some of their books too but warn him that he will not understand them. These books are small and cannot match the bulk and volume of *Valley of Dolls* and Billy is unable to understand the language but he can see that the novel consists of 'clumps of symbols with stars in between'. He is told that the clumps function something like telegrams, with each clump being a message about a situation or a scene. But the clumps are read simultaneously and not sequentially as chapters are in an earthling novel of the ordinary sort: "There isn't any particular relationship between all the messages except that the author has chosen them carefully, so that, when seen all at once they produce an image of life that is beautiful and surprising and deep" (*SHV*, 76).

Slaughterhouse Five is an approximation of this type of novel. Its chapters are divided into short sections (clumps), seldom more than a few paragraphs long. The time tripping both by Billy and the narrator produces an effect somewhat like that achieved in a Tralfamadorian novel i.e. to see many moments at once. The Tralfamadorian scheme enables Vonnegut to embody a new reality in his novel in contrast to the ups and downs reality of the traditional novel. Critics are of the view that his method accords well with the major changes in the concept of physical reality that have come out of contemporary science. Commenting on the relationship between 20th century physics and recent fiction, the critic Jerry H. Bryant opines:

> "Change, ambiguity and subjectivity thus become ways of defining human reality. Novelist after novelist examines these features and expresses almost universal frustration at being deprived of the old stability of metaphysical reality. In Vonnegut's case however, the Tralfamadorian scheme enables him to overcome the problems of change, ambiguity and subjectivity involved in objectifying the events surrounding the fire-bombing of Dresden and the involvement of Billy Pilgrim and the author in them." (Bryant, 73)

In keeping with these views the structure of the novel appears like an atomic entity as Vonnegut's narrative constantly moves back and forth in time and we see Billy becoming 'his history' and existing all at once as an 'electron', "whirling around the central fact of Dresden, the planes of his orbits constantly interacting towards where he has been and will be" (Lundquist, 74).

Stanley Schatt believes that *Slaughterhouse Five* is constructed very much like *Catch 22*. Just as in that novel Yossarian is compelled to think about Snowden's death, yet finds it too painful and tries to avoid its memory, so too is a reluctant Billy Pilgrim forced to return again and again to the firebombing of Dresden. Only when Yossarian and Billy pilgrim learn to cope with mankind's inhumanity and the horror of war they are able to describe the atrocities they have repressed. Billy constantly retreats from Dresden just before the atrocity is about to take place until he hears a group of optometrists singing the barber shop quartet. This reminds him of the group of German soldiers who had shared the protection of Slaughterhouse numbered Five with the American prisoners during the bombing. When Kilgore Trout, Vonnegut's science-fiction writer (who makes an appearance in this novel like many of his other novels) observes Billy's strange expression, he asks Billy if he 'is looking through a time window'. Although Billy denies it, he is doing just that and his observation or recall of the past represents the climax of Vonnegut's novel since it is only after Billy has faced the past that he is able to return to Dresden and live through the Holocaust once more.

Peter J. Reed is of the view that there are certain unifying elements in the novel. The autobiographical first chapter is connected to the last chapter when the author repeats certain details from his life in this chapter as well so as to integrate the frame of the novel with the main narrative. All the events portrayed in the novel are carefully interconnected and events from 'separate times' are often juxtaposed commenting on one another. The prologue to the first chapter and the quick general guidelines to Billy's life in the second, provide the reader with a strong sense of direction. Reed believes that the novel is quite well formed and even has a climax i.e. the execution of Edgar Derby.

Kurt Vonnegut like Joseph Heller believes in the meaninglessness of existence in an absurd world thus approximating the theory of Existentialism. Modern warfare is absurd because of its possibility of absolute annihilation, and therefore the human condition has become absurd and terrifying.

War is an example of man's greatest folly, his inhumanity and his incapacity to maintain an ordered control over his destiny. As a result, Man is locked into a condition he can neither tolerate nor change, a situation, which ultimately destroys and defeats him. Madness, neurosis and eccentricity have become an integral part of Man's circumstance and very often the individual becomes peripheral from society and progressively experiences a growing sense of futility. In consonance with these ideas Billy Pilgrim feels alienated from his environment and for this purpose escapes to Tralfamadore in order to 're-invent' himself.

The narrative technique used by Vonnegut in *Slaughterhouse Five*, is in keeping with the ideas of Existentialism and devices of metafiction. The form of the novel avoids the climax and denouement typical of linear narration as the author frames his story around a nonlinear and circular narration and informs his readers that a writer cannot separate his narration of the story from the story itself. In chapter 1 Vonnegut has already explained this problem to the reader, wondering how he should begin writing his work of fiction about a dreadful reality. After he has finished narrating the story of Dresden once again he directly addresses the reader posing another problem before his audience: now he does not know how to end his work of fiction. The novel ends with an inane and meaningless expression 'Poo-tee-Weet' with the author reiterating once again that nothing intelligent can be said about a carnage like Dresden.

As part of his narrative technique Vonnegut uses the device of intrusion despite creating a narrative distance between himself and his protagonist from the first chapter onward. He interrupts the third person narrative several times to speak in the first person and to tell the reader 'I was there'. T.N. Dhar, commenting upon these intrusions calls this technique Vonnegut's 'leap within' while David Lodge calls this device the technique of 'leapfrogging'. Dhar believes that these intrusions do not jar or surprise the reader but on the contrary lend credibility to Vonnegut's assertion that his experience of Dresden was a lived nightmare. The critic further opines that his leapfrogging is indicative of his passionate urgency in conveying his horror and dislike of war.

The concept of time is important as Billy keeps travelling or 'tripping' back and forth in time, during the course of the novel. The novel contains phases of the life of Billy Pilgrim arranged in non-linear time scheme and all the events in his life are described in a disorderly manner. It is constructed by the inter-lapping of these events that goes to and fro for a span of almost fifty-four years i.e. from Billy's birth in 1922 to his death in 1976. Billy's time travelling begins in chapter two. In this chapter Billy travels to 1944 remembering the Battle of Bulge and his capture by the German forces in the thick Ardennes forest. Chapter four once again takes Billy to the episode of his imprisonment and this time he relives the moment when German photographers clicked pictures of the POWs. In chapters seven and eight Billy actually travels to the future, foreseeing his own death at the hands of the murderer hired by Paul Lazzaro. The device perhaps should not be taken literally for as has been mentioned it symbolizes Billy's disturbed state of mind since Billy actually travels beyond the end of his own life, and is able to predict the time of his own death. Billy's time travelling serves to draw a distinction between external time, which passes in the real world and internal time, which passes in the mind of the character. Vonnegut explores this idea in the novel by referring to quotations by the French thinker Louis Ferdinand Celine who was of the view that the passage of internal time is inextricably linked to the psyche of the individual whereas external time is linked to the world of clocks and calendars. Celine also believed that if time could be stopped then no one would die.

Time travel serves another purpose which is integral to Vonnegut's narrative: these sequences serve as expository flashbacks as the author tells us his protagonist's story going back to the most traumatic event in his life. The shifts in time and the frequent digression from the story of Billy Pilgrim's capture by the Germans serves another purpose for Vonnegut—it conveys the wide gap between the horrifying events of the 20th century and man's inability to comprehend it. Time has not taught human beings any lesson. Unable to learn from Dresden, Nagasaki and Hiroshima Man still continues to commit atrocities.

The Tralfamadorian concept of time is also revealed in the novel. The Tralfamadorians draw the analogy of 'bugs caught in amber' to explain the concept of human beings caught in time. However, these aliens look at everything in the 'fourth dimension', which is free from time itself. The Tralfamadorians believe that all moments of time keep occurring and recurring simultaneously and endlessly and death too is a moment amidst all the other moments. On this planet, Billy learns the new meaning of death, for the perpetual existence of all moments of time removes the negation of death. However the earthlings, unlike the Tralfamadorians believe in 'free will', something that the aliens negate. The aliens are fatalistic and believe that wars will continue on Earth, there is no way to stop them and human beings should accept this harsh reality.

Repetition of events is an integral part of the author's non-linear narration and is used in order to emphasize his anti-war theme. The firebombing of Dresden is repeated over and over again in the novel, as are the numerous deaths, which occur, imparting a cyclical quality to it. The phrase 'so it goes' is repeated a number of times especially when a death takes place. This phrase has been used like a chorus by the author in order to remind his readers that death is omnipresent and in the modern world war torn world has become a triviality:

> "There were hundreds of corpse mines operating by and by. They didn't smell bad at first. But then the bodies rotted and liquefied, and the stink was like roses and mustard gas. So it goes. The Maori Billy had worked with died of the dry heaves after having been ordered to go down in that stink and work. He tore himself to pieces throwing up and throwing up. So it goes." (*SHV*, 185)

In addition to all these devices Vonnegut employs the technique of stream of consciousness and interior monologue to show that all of Billy's thoughts lead indirectly, yet ultimately to Dresden and to the disturbing question as to why man destroys and kills. Billy is always asking himself the same question over and over again—why does man kill what rationale can he possibly have to explain his actions during war.

In 1960s and 1970s the genre of science fiction became extremely popular with a proliferation of novels about aliens visiting the Earth and attempting to establish communications with its inhabitants. An exhaustive discussion of this genre of writing would be quite outside the purview of this work so it would be appropriate to focus on how Vonnegut uses science fiction in his novel and to what purpose. Critics and reviewers have dubbed Kurt Vonnegut as a science fiction novelist but the author himself was skeptical of this epithet stating in an article that this term was applied to his fiction when he wrote a novel called *Player Piano* based on a power struggle between Man and machines. Subsequently his other novels like *Cat's Cradle* and *Sirens of Titans* were also labelled as science fiction and fantasy. Critics are of the view that Vonnegut uses fantasy and science fiction to examine the horror and absurdities of modern civilization and his chaotic fictional world abounds in wonder, coincidence, randomness and irrationality. Science fiction helps lend form to the presentation of this worldview without imposing a falsifying causality upon it.

Slaughterhouse Five is not an out and out science fiction novel. Elements of fantasy and science fiction have been woven in the narrative in order to highlight the plight of modern individuals who like Billy Pilgrim are not sure whether they are living in the past or the future. Writing the novel like a work of science fiction seems a means of escape. Whenever Billy feels stressed, or whenever he thinks about the war and Dresden, he escapes to the alien planet. The Tralfamadorians are kind and do their best to treat Billy with understanding. The technique of science fiction used by the author dramatizes the general condition of man in an absurd universe, captured metaphorically and literally in the Dresden episode and expresses the inevitable desire to escape at least momentarily from such a vision of reality.

The device of Black Humour has been used to emphasize the helplessness of human beings when faced with absurd situations like war. The universe of Kurt Vonnegut's novels is a hostile and ridiculous one, in which a sense of humour is necessary in order to survive. Klinkowitz however is of the opinion that Vonnegut cannot be classified with traditional Black Humourists like Terry Southern, Bruce Jay Freedman or even Joseph Heller. His humour can be defined as 'gallows humour', the humour of people who are laughing in the midst of helplessness especially when they are confronted with death. In other words, the human condition in this world has become so desperate that crying very often does not help and saturated, human beings resort to laughter. Laughter is a response to the frustration of human desires and schemes, as human beings try to bring about a sense of order in a disordered world. The subversion of linear time is a technique which helps Vonnegut make a free play of humour and horror.

Billy story is told in short paragraphs of hundred and fifty pages comprising ten chapters. The horror of wartime realities is juxtaposed with Billy's naive, farcical life as an optometrist, which serves the purpose of a comic interlude. Billy's life as an optometrist produces some of the funniest passages in *Slaughterhouse Five*. For instance one of the details he gives us about Billy's childhood is that even though Billy was not a Catholic there was a gruesome crucifix hanging on the wall of his bedroom. Vonnegut explains that Billy's mother developed a powerful longing for a crucifix. So when she found one she liked in a shop she immediately bought it.

> "She did develop a terrific hankering for a crucifix. And she bought one from a Santa Fe gift shop during a trip the little family made out West during the Great Depression. Like so many Americans, she was trying to construct a life that made sense.... And the crucifix went up on the wall of Billy Pilgrim." (*SHV*, 33)

Although Billy's mother's obsession is mocked at on a serious note, Vonnegut seems to convey the idea that even religion cannot provide protection against war. Through the crucifix, the author also reiterates his belief about wars being a Children's Crusade because the word 'crusade' is derived from 'crux', which means a cross. The bullet proof Bible that Roland Weary carries on his person arouses a great deal of mirth but this religious text does not protect him from death.

In Chapters two, three and four Billy's time travelling arouses laughter, so do his trips to Tralfamadore and his encounter with the actress Montana Wildhack. But underlying this laughter is a grim seriousness as these frivolous details are juxtaposed with the horrifying wartime descriptions of Billy's capture and his experiences in Dresden. The journey of the POWs is described in a humorous vein with Vonnegut mocking at the hobo who continuously reiterates 'this ain't so bad' but the hobo's death due to starvation fills the reader with horror.

However, *Slaughterhouse Five* is not as funny as *Catch 22*. The novel also lacks the humour that is present in Vonnegut's novels like *God Bless You, Mr. Rosewater* and *Mother Night*. The Dresden horror, under any circumstance cannot be portrayed humorously and thus Vonnegut uses only limited humour in the novel.

Parody is a device used by novelists to mock at other literary works for humorous, satirical and ironic effect. Vonnegut uses this device in the novel as he makes numerous literary allusions, parodying and mocking them. The name Billy is reminiscent of the innocent hero of Herman Melville's *Billy Budd*. Pilgrim is suggestive of John Bunyan's seventeenth century moralistic novel *Pilgrim's Progress* in which the hero called Christian encounters many adventures and setbacks on his journey from the world of sin to the foot of the cross, where he finds salvation. Billy too passes through absurd scenes of modern life to find happiness among aliens from outer space. The scene in the Ardennes Forest where Billy and Roland Weary are captured parodies the conclusion of the medieval French epic poem 'The Song of Roland', a war tale in which the protagonist and his best friend die heroically defending Western i.e. Christian civilization against the attack by Muslim Saracens. The Medieval Roland has a horn that he refuses to blow until he gets into serious trouble while Weary has a whistle that he will not blow until he is promoted to a Corporal. The Roland of the Medieval poem is a true Christian, fighting the non-believing Saracean Muslims and Weary is a foot soldier battling the Nazis, the modern day infidels.

To conclude, World War II had a profound impact on Kurt Vonnegut's psyche. The Allied firebombing of Dresden was an atrocity of such magnitude that for two long decades the author kept the horrible memories bottled up inside him not revealing anything to the world. In this respect his feelings were similar to that correspondent of *London Times* who visited Belsen, the Nazi concentration camp along with the Allied troops in April 1945. As the British troops marched into Belsen, the first Nazi concentration camp to be exposed to the world scrutiny they discovered over forty thousand malnourished and dying prisoners and more than ten thousand corpses, rotting in open spaces. The hastily retreating Germans had even robbed human beings the dignity in death by denying them a decent burial. The correspondent began his dispatch thus: "It is my duty to describe something beyond the imagination of mankind." The discovery of Belsen was followed by the discovery of other such camps at Sobibor and Auschwitz and all of them revealed a saga of atrocity that is beyond human imagination. Vonnegut faced a similar problem as the one faced by the correspondent—the increasing gap between the horror of life in the modern world and our imaginative ability (or lack of it) to comprehend its full actuality.

War is a constant, recurring theme in Vonnegut's novels and he especially lays stress on human suffering caused by war. Vonnegut is skeptical of science and technology and expresses a fear that a misuse of technology will bring Doomsday closer. The only way in which this world can be saved is by the commitment of individual human beings to the task of finding a way to resist the destructive immoral forces and assuming the responsibility of becoming better human beings.

Conclusion

7

War has been a compelling subject in literature. Over the years, the American novelist has continuously and consistently criticized war as absurd and insane. Stephen Crane in his novel *The Red Badge of Courage* castigated the Civil War because it caused immense suffering. Half a century later, the country was once again involved in yet another mammoth conflict, the First World War. This war required Americans to curtail their individual freedom in order to assist the nation in attaining victory over their enemies. One of the biggest assaults on individual freedom was the conscription or the compulsory drafting of young men into the army. Local boards were formed to implement the draft so that the role of the government in the resulting loss of liberty was disguised. The First Great War caused colossal death and destruction and novelists like Ernest Hemingway, Dos Passos, Thomas Boyd and E.E. Cummings who had participated in the war wrote about the endless suffering caused by combat. Some of them like Dos Passos and Hemingway even suggested ways to escape the insanity of warfare. Passos' hero John Andrews in his *Three Soldiers* deserts the army and 'makes a separate peace' and so does Hemingway's Frederic Henry who escapes to Switzerland with his beloved Catherine, turning his back on dehumanizing warfare.

In 1954 Malcolm Cowley wrote in the *Literary Situation* that in comparison to World War I many more novels have been written about World War II (Cowley, 34). The novels of this period reflect the plight of the individuals in modern industrialized societies where human beings are considered as mere commodities. Thus, the battlefields of the twentieth century have provided some of America's best authors with fertile ground in which to sow the seeds of their concern about the plight of the individual besieged by the mass culture of the modern technological society. Technology in the 21st century is continuously shrinking the Earth and forcing Mankind into more intimate awareness and interdependence. War has been virtually incessant during recorded human history but in the contemporary age due to the ingenuity of modern technology we are instantly aware of every minor skirmish and major encounter around the world. War with its destructive potential expanded to the indefinable limits of technology has become a logical metaphor for the plight of civilized society in the modern world.

The novelists examined in the present work were all combatants who used the battlefield experience as a means of debunking combat. These writers express the opinion that war, the absolutism of the army causes depersonalization of man, and modern technology threatens to obliterate the individual's very existence. They express a concern for the survival of man threatened by the violence of the modern world. However, despite projecting a grim scenario, these novelists express the hope that the scourge of war may be eradicated from the world. The solution for elimination of war is the personal choice of each and every human being and as citizens of the world individuals must act in a responsible manner. The novelists are of the view that unquestioning obedience of people towards their state and country is sometimes not true patriotism but often an act of irresponsibility, especially when the country forces its people to adhere to its war mongering policies. The novelists examined in the study urge us not to get involved with such barbarian societies or states. Instead, they ask us to be responsible towards one another as men and women of this world and not of particular nations only. Each of the novels provides some solution, albeit skeptical for the abolition of wars from this world.

Chapter 1 of this work outlines the causes and factors responsible for the development of the war novel as a genre in

American fiction. The war and combat novel emerged as a distinctive genre due to the prevailing social, political, and literary climate of America in the years immediately following the Second World War. The war had transformed America into an economic and political giant but the war novelists were primarily adversary novelists who did not see America as the land of plenty and prosperity where every individual had the opportunity to fulfill his or her dream. With memories of the depredation caused by the war deeply etched on their mind, these writers strongly chastised the American leaders for dragging the nation into war and were especially critical of the army, which was perceived by them as a totalitarian institution.

In the context of music, the word 'absurd' originally meant 'out of harmony'. The dictionary defines the word as incongruous, unreasonable, and illogical. Thus absurdity prevails when reason does not function. Reason on the other hand guides man and makes him conscious of what is right and just and it also makes him assert himself in a given situation. Thus the war novels of Joseph Heller and Kurt Vonnegut portray a war-ravaged world that is absurd and insane. In this irrational and illogical world, the nature of reality too came to be questioned with post-modernist writers like John Barth and Ronald Sukenick debating whether realism could effectively depict the insanity and chaos of the modern world. In consonance with their ideas novelists like Kurt Vonnegut and Joseph Heller eschewed realism and made use of devices like Black Humour, Non-linear Narration, Parody and Self-Reflexivity in order to portray their revulsion of war. While these writers turned their back on realism, novelists like James Jones and Norman Mailer continued to write in the Naturalistic-Realistic tradition in their depiction of war and combat. Jones and Mailer in the tradition of the Naturalists conceived their novels as vehicles of social protest where the army became a metaphor for the rapacious American capitalist society. The writers not only depict brutal hand-to-hand combat in the vast, infernal forests of the Pacific Islands but also warn against the latent dangers of conflict and the impact of war on the civilian population of a country. Many of these novelists portray the anomie, fear, paranoia and despair of soldiers who are involved in combat.

Chapter 2 is an analysis of James Jones's war trilogy *From Here to Eternity*, *The Thin Red Line*, and *Whistle*. The central theme in the novels of Jones is the depersonalization of man caused by the war and the institution that fights the war i.e. the army. Jones's first novel *From Here to Eternity* is essentially a study of the struggle of the individual to maintain some semblance of integrity without being swallowed up by the system i.e. the army. The second novel in the trilogy focuses on ferocious combat in the jungles of Philippines. Here too the lives of the soldiers have no value and they simply become 'parts' of the war machine, cogs in the wheel, and when one 'part' stops functioning it is merely replaced by another. The soldiers cannot display any individuality during actual combat, as they have to mechanically obey the orders of the superior officers, as this is necessary for their own survival as well as the survival of their unit or Company. Jones's last novel in the trilogy *Whistle*, focuses on the disintegration of the human being who has become a soldier. While in the army, the individual is trained as a true soldier, and is then sent to the battlefront to fight a war. After having witnessed and participated in mortal conflict the soldier cannot adjust to civilian life, for memory of the violence and bloodshed of the battlefield continue to haunt him all his life. The soldier having lost his personal identity and with a battered psyche collapses mentally and physically. This is what happens to Winch, Landers, Strange and Prell, the four characters of *Whistle*.

In all the three novels, Jones expresses the fear that the army might become too powerful after the war and this may endanger individual liberty. However, despite the fact that Jones is critical of this organization there are subtle suggestions in the three novels that perhaps the depersonalization caused by the army is necessary for fighting wars successfully. If each individual asserts his will, the discipline of this organization would be breached and survival during combat would become impossible. This is the reason why individuals like Warden compromise, while idealists like Prewitt suffer.

Jones's vision of the world is extremely bleak and pessimistic but he offers hope to Mankind through the character of Prewitt. Prewitt's fight with the system, his obdurate refusal to support the life negating policies of the army is a lesson for all individuals. If human beings refuse to support despotism and tyranny then wars will certainly disappear from this Earth. It is true that Prewitt dies but at least he shows the world a way of resistance through the path of courage and honesty.

Chapter 3 is devoted to an analysis of Norman Mailer's first novel *The Naked and the Dead*. War in this novel has been looked upon as an outcome of inexorable conditions prevailing in modern society. The author, closely observing the American society comes to the conclusion that this society is essentially corrupt, it destroys all ideals and breeds a totalitarian instinct. Its fascist structure induces a craving for power and this results in incessant warfare.

In the novel Mailer debunks combat and warns against the dormant dangers of war rather than providing a graphic description of fighting and suffering caused by violence and destruction (although he does dwell upon the bestial nature of men at war). The war had transformed America into a superpower and Mailer feared that the country's insatiable hunger for power would lead to many wars in the future as well. Mailer's novel is a scathing comment on America's hypocrisy. Although the country claimed to be a democracy this was only on the surface for ultimately, the nation would adopt a policy of aggrandizement and follow a course of Neo Imperialism which would prove to be detrimental for other countries in future. Despite the fact that the Second World War is a specific and figurative context of *The Naked and the Dead*, the novel has very little to say about the military enemy, the Japanese, whose forces led by General Toyaku, need to be overcome if the Americans are to take the Island of Anopopei. No attempt is made to write about the international nature of war as there are very few allusions to Japan (the single Japanese character Wakara is given only a few pages), and Germany and Italy are mentioned only in passing reference. Mailer is concerned with the enemy within, the totalitarian army and power hungry military commanders who would continue to plunge the country into conflict to justify and strengthen their existence. Mailer's contention proved to be true as in the 1950s and 1960s America waged wars against Korea and Vietnam and his novel *Why Are We In Vietnam?* questioned the American government's aims in fighting a war in this country.

The author conceived his novel in the tradition of the Naturalists revealing that modern man is entrapped by biological and social determinism but *The Naked and the Dead* is not totally without hope and Mailer does not permit fascist, totalitarian and despotic forces a clear victory in the novel as both Cummings and Croft (symbols of tyranny) are thwarted by the absurdities of chance. Although liberals like Hearn and Red too are defeated, the author seems to suggest that individuals do possess the potential to challenge authority and autocracy. Once again the question of personal disobedience is raised. If the citizens of a country do not support the war mongering policies of its leaders, wars will definitely be abolished.

The Americans took a step in this direction when the country invaded Vietnam and President Lyndon Jonhson began massive bombardment of North Vietnam in 1965. At this juncture the anti-Vietnam war movement began in America and gained momentum after a law passed by the Supreme Court, which decreed that government was authorized to compulsorily conscript young men to fight the war in Vietnam. As a result boys merely in their teens were sent to the alien land. The government's policies led to a large number of casualties as the country's youth began to die in the line of fire. Once this happened the citizens of America began demanding answers to the nation's war aims in Vietnam as questions like 'what are we fighting for?' began to be raised. The university and college campuses reverberated with slogans like 'Draft Beer not boys', 'Make love not war', 'One, two, three four, we do not want your stinking war', and 'Hell no we won't go'. The students began to defy the compulsory conscription decree and many of them left for Canada. Activists, writers, celebrities and musicians began to participate in these protests and their writing, music and speeches reflected the anger and hopelessness that the

Americans felt over the war. Historians argue that the anti-war protests had a significant impact on the length and perhaps the outcome of the Vietnam War. The Iraq war was followed by large-scale protests in both Britain and America, as the citizens of both these countries did not want the wars to be fought. This is the kind of challenge to authority that Mailer was advocating in his novel. As responsible individuals the citizens of a country must question the government and its policies because ultimately the responsibility for the abolition of war should lie with the people themselves.

Chapter 4 is an analysis of Irwin Shaw's novel *The Young Lions*. The novel is set against the backdrop of war in Europe and is an example of historical fiction with the author using historical episodes and battles like the Normandy Landings, the London Blitzkrieg, Occupation and Liberation of Paris, Battle of El Alamein and Battle of Britain as a background for the action of its story. The central conflict of *The Young Lions* is a moral one: would virtue ultimately defeat vice in this corrupt, degenerate world? Shaw's novel is therefore a moral allegory of good versus evil. Christian Diestel represents evil in the novel while Noah Ackerman and Michael Whitacre are symbolic of good. Shaw reveals that for individuals like Diestel who do not possess strong moral values to begin with, evil holds a special attraction. Malevolence has a power and all human beings are drawn to it but Faust like Diestel wilfully chooses evil over good, succumbing to its attraction absolutely and completely. However in the battle between good and evil, good triumphs when Michael kills Christian. Shaw's novel offers the hope that wars can be abolished from this Earth if humane people rule the world and Michael and Captain Green are those human beings who will make the world a better place. Noah also dies with this hope deeply ingrained in his soul. One day, human beings will heal the world and make it a better place for the entire human race, and when this happens there will be no more wars on Earth.

Chapter 5 is an analysis of Joseph Heller's novel *Catch 22*. Heller looks upon war as absurd and insane and like Mailer projects the despotic army as the enemy within. This analysis of the institution is based on the author's personal experience as he exposes the army's true nature in *Catch 22*. Exploding the myth that the army is an institution where order and discipline reign supreme, Heller shows this organization as inefficient, selfish and corrupt governed by ridiculous and ambiguous laws like Catch 22 that ensnare the wretched individual in their circular reasoning. In the novel, no individual can win against the diktat of the army.

Heller consciously and forthrightly uses war as a metaphor for modern industrialized society admitting as much in an interview: "*Catch 22* is about contemporary, regimented business society depicted against the background of universal sorrow and inevitable death that is the lot of all of us" (*Replies*, 30). The society depicted in *Catch 22* is absurd and frightening because it deprives the individual of dignity and leads him towards destruction. It is this absurd world that Yossarian ultimately decides to desert and his desertion can be interpreted as an act of responsibility. His forsaking the army and the war is an act of valour and offers hope to man trapped by the insanity of the modern world. *Catch 22* teaches us that as individuals we can make a moral choice once again through a method of personal disobedience. This would be an effective weapon against war because war is a consequence of people mindlessly obeying the political and social machinery of their country. Therefore, human beings have to learn the lesson of resistance and evasion if they intend to abolish war from the face of the Earth.

Chapter 6 is devoted to a study of Kurt Vonnegut's Dresden novel *Slaughterhouse Five*. The author lays great stress on the suffering caused by war and comes to the conclusion that human life has no value in a world plagued by conflict. This is perhaps the reason why countries engaged in wars resort to bombing of civilian targets. This was the strategy adopted both by the Allied and Axis powers during the Second World War. The Axis powers resorted to heavy bombing of the city of London and the Allies retorted by bombing cities in Italy and Germany. Each attack was followed by a counter attack. When the Japanese refused surrender, the Allies unleashed the terror of the nuclear bomb on the civilian population of Hiroshima and Nagasaki. The author shows the moral degeneration of military men and political leaders who falsely tried to justify the Dresden raid on the grounds that the German city was strategically important for the Allies and therefore had to be bombed. In actuality, the strategic significance of the city was 'scarcely marginal' and yet military Commanders like Britain's Air Chief Marshall Arthur Harris resorted to indiscriminate bombing of the city. Vonnegut views this as a blatant support of violence.

Slaughterhouse Five upholds the idea that wars are a by-product of moral degeneration as human beings have lost traditional values like kindness, sympathy, and compassion. One of the reasons for moral corruption of man is the loss of religious values. The author reveals in the novel that how Billy Pilgrim keeps the crucifix given to him by his mother merely as a 'prize' and not as a holy object to remind him of the Christian values of benevolence and compassion. Vonnegut shows great skepticism towards science and technology, for science he believes has increased man's brutishness and destroyed his compassion. The author himself was a witness to the destruction caused by modern technology, which within a span of fourteen hours annihilated a city that was thousands of years old.

The author is highly critical of individuals who display a great apathy and indifference towards war and violence that have saturated the contemporary world. All human beings living in the modern world have become desensitized towards cruelty, sadism and brutality as newspapers and electronic media inundate us daily with news of massacres happening around the world. In *Slaughterhouse Five* Billy is the modern day Everyman who has developed an apathetic attitude towards the violent activities of the contemporary world. He has even found an escape route and flees to Tralfamadore whenever he is compelled to think of Dresden and other massacres.

Despite the fact that Vonnegut believes in the moral degeneration of man, he is hopeful like Irwin Shaw that one day human beings will learn to be kind and eradicate war from this Earth. Although there is no symbolic gesture of affirmation in

Vonnegut's novel (as there was in Heller's) the author believes that human beings can definitely act to change the condition and quality of life on earth. He does not want to believe in the Tralfamadorian view that it is pointless to find a cure for wars that plague the Earth and wants to 'poison' the minds of his readers with humanity.

The phrase has been coined by Vonnegut himself and he desires to 'catch' men before they become Colonels and Generals and encourage them to become better human beings. Like Heller and Mailer, Vonnegut too advocates the method of personal disobedience to resist aggression and warfare. He gives the readers his own example—he has asked his children never to participate in any war or support any form of violence. Vonnegut expects his readers to do the same, at the same time expressing the hope that one day man will give up his greed and the innate goodness and decency of human beings will help in preventing wars.

Novelists like Jones and Mailer depict a belligerent, all male world in their novels. During combat a soldier becomes a killer and a brutal wielder of power and awakens to the primitive elements lying in the hidden recesses of his nature. However this excessively masculine world of men without women is a tragic one because it is plagued by unredeemed brutality and butchery from which there is no escape. This aggressively 'masculine' war torn world awakens the sleeping bestiality within human beings and Jones, Mailer, Shaw and Vonnegut focus on the animal nature of man during war.

This is not just a figment of their imagination but is corroborated by facts. History tells us the story of millions of people killed during Second World War. Films and books about the holocaust expose the fact that men become subhuman during a conflict and there are numerous episodes of cruelty and torture associated with this war. However, the Second World War is distant memory for the contemporary world since it was fought in the middle of last century. Nevertheless, violence and bestiality continued in subsequent wars as well as Man repeatedly revealed his animal nature inflicting torment and pain on his fellow human beings.

There are chilling accounts of violence and bloodshed perpetrated as the print and the electronic media had made considerable progress in the latter half of the 20th century and in 1971 one of the worst episodes of butchery occurred when the American GI's murdered hundreds of innocent civilians of Vietnam in the region called Mylai. The slaughter was given exhaustive coverage by the media and shocked the world. More recently, the insanity of human beings during war was revealed after the Iraq aggression when photographs of British and American soldiers torturing POWs at the Abu Gharib prison were splashed in all the leading newspapers of the world. Once again the conflict in Iraq revealed the grisly and macabre nature of war.

While writing the preface of his novel *War and Remembrance* Herman Wouk stated that the essence of war lies in remembrance. Wouk writes that:

> "War is an old habit of thought, an old frame of mind, an old political technique, that must now pass as human sacrifice and human slavery have passed. I have faith that the human spirit will prove equal to the long and heavy task of ending war. Against the pessimistic mood of our time, I think that the human spirit—for all its dark side that I here portray is in essence heroic...the beginning of the end of war lies in remembrance." (Wouk, i)

Literature on war has tried to remind us time and again that war is a catastrophe and must be avoided at all costs. It is true that perhaps no work of art can portray the real war and the real anguish of people who suffered and the poet Whitman while writing about the Civil War expressed this doubt when he said that the real war will never get into the books and no individual experience as reported in literature can do justice to it.

Nevertheless the war novelist has tried to express his angst and get the 'real' war into their novels. It is time that men learn from their mistakes and perhaps war literature can play an important role in preventing history from repeating itself.

However, violence and war have continued throughout the twentieth and twenty-first centuries. In 1999 war was brought to our drawing rooms as we witnessed the ferocious battle for Tiger Hill as many of our soldiers perished during the Kargil aggression. In 2003 once again the world trembled with fear as the American armies stepped into the Middle East to crush a belligerent Iraq and a world conflict seemed imminent. Today with most countries having amassed nuclear weapons war could begin at the press of a button and the world could end with the blink of an eye. The next war would end in absolute annihilation. Let us then lend an ear to the impassioned plea of the war novelist—a plea for peace and abolition of wars from Earth.

Bibliography

PRIMARY SOURCES

Heller, Joseph. *Catch 22*. Great Britain: Vintage, 1962.

——, *Something Happened*. Knopf, 1974.

——, *Good as Gold*. Simon & Schuster, 1979.

——, *Closing Time*. Simon & Schuster, 1994.

Jones, James. *From Here to Eternity*. New York: Scribner's, 1951.

——, *The Thin Red Line*. New York: Scribner's, 1962.

——, *Whistle*. New Delhi: Rupa & Co., 1979.

——, *WW II*. New York: Grosset and Dunpalap, 1975.

Mailer, Norman. *The Naked and the Dead*. USA: Holt, Rinehart and Winston, 1948.

——, *Barbary Shore*. New York: Rinehart, 1951.

——, *The Deer Park*. New York: Putnam's, 1967.

——, *Why are We in Vietnam?* New York: Putnam's, 1967.

Shaw, Irwin. *The Young Lions*. New York: Random House, 1948.

Vonnegut, Kurt. *Slaughterhouse Five or The Children's Crusade or a Duty Dance With Death*. Great Britain: Jonathan Cape Ltd., 1970.

——, *Player Piano*. New York: Delta, 1952.

——, *Wampeters, Foma and Gramfallons*. New York: Delta, 1975.

Wouk, Herman. *War and Remembrance*. New York: Little Brown & Co., 1985.

SECONDARY SOURCES

Books

Aaron, Daniel. *Writers on the Left: Episodes in American Literary Communism, (Communism in American Life)*. New York: Harcourt, 1961.

Adams, Laura. *Existential Battles: The Growth of Norman Mailer*. Athens, OH: Ohio University Press, 1976.

Aichinger, Peter. *The American Soldier in Fiction, 1880 – 1963: A History of Attitudes Toward Warfare and the Military Establishment*. Ames: Iowa State University Press, 1975.

Aldridge, John W. *After the Lost Generation: A Critical Study of the Writers of Two Wars*. New York: Noonday Press, 1951.

Arendt, Hannah. *The Origins of Totalitarianism*. New Edition. New York: Harcourt, 1966.

Becker, George. *Documents of Modern Literary Realism*. Princeton: Princeton University Press, 1963.

Bryant, Jerry H. *The Open Decision: The Contemporary American Novel and Its Intellectual Background*. New York: Free Press, 1970.

Burgess Anthony. *The Novel Now: A Guide to Contemporary Fiction*. UK: Norton, 1967.

Carter, Steven R. *James Jones: An American Literary Orientalist Master*. Urbana: University of Illinois Press, 1998.

Christie, Paul. *The Beleaguered Individual: A Study of Twentieth Century American Novels*. PhD. Thesis. University of Tennessee, 2001.

Cowley, Malcolm. *The Literary Situation*. New York, 1954.

Culmer, John. *From Coleridge to Catch 22: Image of Society*. London: Macmillan, 1980.

Dewey, John. *Individualism: Old and New*. New York: Minton, Balch, 1930.

Ehrilch, Robert. *Norman Mailer: The Radical as Hipster*. Metuchen, NS: Scarecrow Press, 1978.

Eisinger, Chester. *Fiction of the Forties*. Chicago: University of Chicago Press, 1963.

Ekrich, Arthur A., Jr. *The Decline of American Liberalism*. New York: Longman, 1955.

Frankland, Noble. *Bomber Offensive: The Devastation of Europe*. New York: Ballentine, 1971.

Fusell, Paul. *The Great War and Modern Memory*. New York: Oxford University Press, 1975.

Giles, James R. *James Jones*. Twayne United States Authors Series. Boston: Twayne, 1981.

——, *Irwin Shaw*. Twayne United States Authors Series. Boston: Twayne, 1984.

Goldsmith, David. *Fantasist of Fire and Ice*. Bowling Green USA: Bowling Green Press, 1972.

Gordon, Andrew. *An American Dreamer: A Psychoanalytic Study of the Fiction of Norman Mailer*. Rutherford: Fairleigh Dickinson University Press, 1980.

Gutman, Stanley T. *Mankind in Barbary: The Individual and Society in the Novels of Norman Mailer*. Hanover, NH: University Press of New England, 1975.

Harper, Howard M. *Desperate Faith: A Study of Bellow, Salinger, Mailer, Baldwin and Updike*. USA: The University of North Press, Chappell Hill, 1967.

Harris, William H. and Judith S. Levy, Ed. *The New Columbia Encyclopedia*. New York: Columbia University Press, 1975.

Hassan, Ihab. *Radical Innocence: Studies on the Contemporary American Novel*. Princeton: Princeton University Press, 1961.

Heath, Jim. *Decade of Disillusionment: The Kennedy-Johnson Years*. Indiana: Bloomington, 1975.

Hodgson, Godfrey. *America in Our Time*. Garden City, New York: Doubleday, 1976.

Hux, S.H. *Myth and Existential Vision*. PhD. Thesis. University of Connecticut.

Irving, David. *The Destruction of Dresden*. New York: Ballentine, 1960.

Jones, Peter G. *War and the Novelist: Appraising the American War Novel*. Columbia, Mo: University of Missouri Press, 1976.

Kahler Eric. *The Tower and the Abyss*. New York, 1967.

Karl Frederick. *American Fictions 1949-1980*. New York: Harper Collins, 1989.

Kazin, Alfred. *Bright Book of Life: American Novelists and Storytellers from Hemingway to Mailer*. Boston: Little Brown, 1971.

Kiley, Frederick and Walter McDonald, Ed. *A Catch 22 Casebook*. New York: Crowell, 1973.

Klinkowitz, Jerome. *The Vonnegut Statement*. Ed. John Somers. Dell Delta: Delacorte Press, 1973.

——, *Reforming the Novel and the World*. Boston: G.K. Hall & Co., 1990.

——, *Vonnegut and the New Novel*. London: Methuen, 1982.

Leeds, Marc. *The Vonnegut Encyclopedia: An Authorized Compendium*. Westport, CT: Greenwood Publishing Group, 1995.

Macshane, Frank. *Into Eternity—The Life of James Jones: American Writer*. Boston: Houghton, 1985.

Merrill, Robert. *Norman Mailer*. Twayne's United States Author's Series. Boston: Twayne, 1978.

Nagel, James Ed. *Critical Essays on Joseph Heller*. Boston: G.K. Hall & Co. 1984.

Older, Raymond M. *Beyond The Wasteland: A Study of the American Novel in the Nineteen Sixties*. New Haven: Yale University Press, 1972.

Page, Norman. *Modern Novelists*. New York: St Martin's, 1995.

Pinsker, Sanford. *Understanding Joseph Heller: Understanding Contemporary American Literature*. Columbia, SC. University of South Carolina Press, 1991.

Pizer, Donald. *Twentieth Century American Literary Naturalism: An Interpretation*. Cross Currents/Modern Critiques/New Series. Carbondale: Southern Illinois, University Press, 1982.

Podhoretz, Norman. *Doings and Undoings: The Fifties and After in American Writing*. New York: Farrar, 1964.

Poirer, Richard. *Modern Masters*. New York: Viking, 1972.

Radford, Jean. *Norman Mailer: A Critical Study*. London: Prentice Hall, 1979.

Riesman, David *et al. The Lonely Crowd: A Study of the Changing American Character*. New Haven: Yale University Press, 1970.

Rouland, Richard and Bradbury Malcolm Ed. *A History of American Literature from Puritanism to Post Modernism*. USA: Penguin, 1992.

Sale, Richard. "An Interview with Joseph Heller". *Studies in the Novel IV*. Boston: G.K. Hall and Co. 1970.

Sartre, Jean Paul. *Being, and Nothingness: A Phenomenological Essay on Ontology*. Trans. Hazel E. Barnes. New York: Washington Square Press, 1956.

Schultz, Max. *Black Humour Fiction in the Sixties: A Pluralistic Definition of Man and His World*. Ohio University Press, 1973.

Shannon, David A. *Between the Wars: America, 1919–1941*. Boston: Houghton, 1965.

Solotaroff, Robert. *Down Mailer's Way*. Urbana: University of Illinois Press, 1974.

Sukenick, Ronald. "*Death of the Novel*". Qtd. by Lundquist in Kurt Vonnegut: Fredrick Ungar, New York, 1980.

Walsh, Jeffrey. *American War Literature: 1914 to Vietnam*. New York: St. Martin's Press, 1982.

Ward, Glenn. *Postmodernism*. Chicago: Contemporary Books, 1997.

Waugh, Patricia. *Metafiction: The Theory and Practice of Self-Conscious Fiction*. www.microsoftreader.com.

Weber Max. *The Protestant Ethic and the Spirit of Capitalism*. Trans. Talcott Parsons. New York: Scribner's, 1958.

Weston, Jessie L. *The Quest of The Holy Grail*. New York: Doubleday, 1975.

Articles

Adams, Richard P. "A Second Look at From Here to Eternity." *College English* 17.4 (Jan. 1956): 205-10.

Aldrich Nelson W. Jr. "The Art of Fiction: James Jones". *Paris Review* 20 (1959): 34-55.

——, "Writers at Work". *Paris Review* 3 (1967): 246-47.

Aldridge John W. "The Last James Jones". *New York Times Book Review* 83.10 (Mar. 5 1978): 1, 30-31.

——, "The War Writers Ten Years Later". *Contemporary Literary Criticism*: V (1974) Detroit: Gale Research Co.: 258.

Algren, Nelson."The Catch". *The Nation* 193 (Nov. 4, 1961): 358.

Bellow, Saul. "Some Notes on Recent American Fiction". *The American Novel Since World War II*. Ed. Marcus Klein. Greenwich, CT: Fawcett, 1969: 159-74.

Blues, Thomas. "The Moral Structure of *Catch 22*". *Studies in the Novel* 3 (1971): 64-79.

Broer, Lawrence. "Sanity Plea". *Schizophrenia in the Novels of Kurt Vonnegut*. London: UNI Book Research, 1989: 88-91.

Brustein, Robert. "The Logic of Survival in a Lunatic World". Nagel: 48-59.

Burg, David F. "The Hero of the Nation and the Dead". *Modern Fiction Studies* 17.3 (Autumn 1971): 387-401.

Burg, Charles. "*Slaughterhouse Five* and the Comforts of Indifference." *Essays in Literature* 7 (Spring 1981): 46-48.

Burhans, Clinton S. "Structural Patterns and Unifying Elements in *Catch 22*". *Twentieth Century Literature* 19 (Oct. 1973): 240-48.

——, "The Best Catch There is". *Modern Fiction Studies* (Summer 1975): 191.

Cantwell, Robert. "Another Eternity". *Newsweek* (Nov. 23, 1953): 107.

Chabot, Barry C. "*Slaughterhouse Five* and the Comforts of Indifferencc". *Essays in Literature* 8 (1981): 45-51.

Clemons, Walter. "Comedy of Fear". *Newsweek* (Oct. 14, 1974): 118.

Cooperman, Stanley. "Aesthetics and the Doom of Individualism". *A Collection of Critical Essays*. Ed. Holger Klein. London: Macmillan, 1976: 23-31.

Crichton, Michael. "Slaughterhouse Five". *The Critic As Artist: Essays on Books, 1920-1970*. New York: Liveright, 1972.

Denniston, Constance. "The American Romance—Parody: A Study of Heller's *Catch 22*". *Emporia State Research Studies* 14.2 (1965): 42-59.

Dhar, T.N. "Vonnegut's Leap Within". *Journal of Indo American Studies* 14 (1984): 40-44.

Epstein, Joseph. "Joseph Heller's Milk Train: Nothing More to Express". *Book World: The Washington Post* (Oct. 6, 1974): 1-2.

Falstein, Louis. "This is the Army". *New Rèpublic* 124 (March 5, 1957): 21.

Fiedler, Leslie A. "James Jones' Dead End Young Werther: The Bum as American Culture Hero". *Commentary* 12.3 (Sept. 1951): 252-55.

Frank, Mike. "Eros and Thanatos". *Canadian Review of American Studies* (1981): 78.

Geismar, Maxwell. "James Jones and the American Novel". *American Moderns from Rebellion to Conformity*. New York: Hill and Wang, 1958.

Gkrouger, Doug. "Time Structure in Catch 22". *Critique* 12.2 (1970): 71-75.

Glicksberg, Charles. "Racial Attitudes in *From Here To Eternity*". *Phylon* 14 (1985): 385.

Green, Daniel. "A World Worth Laughing At: Catch 22 and the Humour of Black Humour". *Studies in the Novel* 27.2 (Summer 1995): 186-96.

Greenfield, Josh. "22 Was Funnier than 14". *New York Times Book Review* (March 1968): 3.

Greiner, Donald J. "Vonnegut's *Slaughterhouse Five* and the Fiction of Atrocity". *Critique* 15.3 (1973): 38-51.

Griffith, Ben Jr. "Rear Rank Robin Hood: James Jones's Folk Hero". *Georgia Review* 10.1 (Spring 1956): 41-46.

Hartshorne, Thomas. "From *Catch 22* to *Slaughterhouse Five*: The Decline of the Political Mode". *South Atlantic Quarterly* 78 (1979): 73-74.

Hasley, Louis. "Dramatic Tension in *Catch 22*". *Midwestern Quarterly* (Winter, 1974). Kansas State College of Pittsburgh: 190.

Hassan, Ihab. "Encounter with Necessity". *Critical Essays on Norman Mailer*. Ed. J. Michael Lennon. *Critical Essays on American Literature*. Boston: G.K. Hall, 1986: 91-98.

Holbling, Walter. "Out of Time and History: Loose Ends of the Mimetic Tradition in the Recent American Novel". *Journal of American Studies* 5 (1980): 53-60.

Horkins, John R. "A Conversation between James Jones and Leslie Hanscome". *James Jones: A Checklist*. Michigan: Gale Research Co., 1974.

Hutcheon, Linda. "Historiographic Metafiction: Parody and the Intertextuality of History". htpp//tspace. library. utoronto.ca/bitstream/1807: 3-10.

Jones, Ernest. "Minority Report". *Nation* 172 (Mar. 17, 1951): 254.

Kar, Praful. "Norman Mailer and the Shift of Fictional Modes". *Indian Journal of American Studies* 14 (July 1984): 44-46.

Karl, Frederick. "Joseph Heller's *Catch 22*: Only Fools Walk in Darkness". *Contemporary American Novelists*. Ed. Harry T. Moore. Crosscurrents/Modern Critiques. Carbondale: Southern Illinois University Press, 1964: 134-42.

Kennard, Jean. "Joseph Heller: At War with Absurdity". *Mosaic* 3 (Spring) University of Marituba: 75-80.

Ketterer, David. "Vonnegut's Spiral Siren: Call From Dresden's Lunar Vistas to Tralfamadore". *New Worlds for Old: The Apocalyptic Imagination, Science Fiction and American Literature*. Bloomington: Indiana University Press, 1974: 300-01.

Klinkowitz, Jerome. "Why They Read Vonnegut". *The Vonnegut Statement*. Ed. John Somers. Dell Delta: Delacorte Press, 1973.

Lardner, John. "Anatomy of the Regular Army". *New Yorker* 27.4 (Mar. 10, 1951): 117-19.

Layman, Richard. "James Jones". *Dictionary of Literary Biography* Vol. II: *American Novelists Since World War II.* Detroit: Gale Research Co., 1978.

Le Chair, Thomas. "*Catch 22*: An Analysis". *Critique* 17.1 (1975): 16-17.

Lifton, Robert J. "Psychoanalysis of Atrocity". Qtd. by Greiner. 44-48.

Lucas, George. "The Ideology of Modernism". Trans. John Mander and Necke Mander. *Twentieth Century Literary Criticism: A Reader*. Ed. David Lodge. London: Longman, 1972: 474-87.

Lundquist, James. "The New Reality of *Slaughterhouse Five*". *Kurt Vonnegut*. Ed. Frederick Ungar. New York. 70-90.

Macauley, Robbie. "Private Jones's Revenge". *Kenyan Review* 13.3 (Summer 1951): 526-29.

Martine, James J. "The Courage to Defy". Nagel. 142-49.

Massent, Peter. "Breakfast of Champions: The Direction of Kurt Vonnegut's Fiction." *Journal of American Studies* 7 (April, 1974): 102-05.

McDonald, Walter. "He Took Off: Yossarian and the Different Drummer." *CEA Critic* 36.4 (1973): 14-16.

Merill, Sam. "Conversations with Joseph Heller". *Literary Conversations Series*. Ed. Adam J. Sorkin. Jackson, MS: University Press of Mississippi, 1993: 144-76.

Merrill, Robert. "Vonnegut's Breakfast of Champions: The Conversion of Heliogablus." *Critique* 18.3 (1977): 5-6.

Michel Michott, Paulette. "Jones's The Thin Red Line: The End of Innocence". *Revove Des Langues Viventes* 30 (1964): 15.

Mitchell, Julian. "Under Mad Gods". Nagel. 32-50.

Mitchell, Lee Clark. "Naturalism and the Languages of Determinism". *Columbia Literary History of the United States*. Ed. Emory Elliot. New York: Columbia University Press, 1988: 525-45.

Mudrick, Marvin. "Mailer and Styron: Guests of the Establishment." *Hudson Review* 17 (Autumn, 1964): 364-65.

Musil, Robert K. "There should be more to love than Death: A Conversation with Kurt Vonnegut." *The Nation* 2 (August, 1980): 128-32.

Muskowitz, Sam. "Explorers of the Infinite". www.scifictionarchive.com: 1-20.

Muste, John M. "Better to Die Laughing: The War Novels of Joseph Heller and John Ashmead." *Critique* 5.2 (Fall 1962): 16-27.

——, "Norman Mailer and John Doss Passos: The Question of Influence". *Modern Fiction Studies* 17.3 (Autumn 1971): 361-74.

Nanda, Bijay K. "Heller's *Catch 22*: The Problem of its Ending". *Indian Journal of American Studies* 22.2 (Summer 1992): 126-30.

Orlowski, Victoria. "Metafiction". www.postmodernist literature.com.:2

Pinsker, Sanford. "Fire and Ice: The Radical Cuteness of Kurt Vonnegut Jr.". *Between Two Worlds: The American Novels in the 1960s*. New York: Whitson, 1980: 1-19.

Reed, Peter J. "The End of the Road: *Slaughterhouse Five* or the Children's Crusade". *Kurt Vonnegut* Jr. University of Minnesota: Warner Books, 1972: 180-94.

Rideout, Walter B. "The Radical Novel in the United States 1900-1954: Some Interrelations of Literature and Society". *President and Fellows of Harvard College* (1956). Harvard University Press: 253-56.

Rolo, Charles. "Irwin Shaw". *Contemporary Literary Criticism* VIII. Detroit: Gale Research Co., 1970.

Rovit, Earl. "Some Shapes in Recent American Fiction". *Contemporary Literature* (Autumn 1974): 550-65.

Schatt, Stanley. "Vonnegut's Dresden Novel *Slaughterhouse Five*." *Kurt Vonnegut*. Boston: G.K. Hall & Co., 1976: 82-100.

Seltzer, Leon F. "Milo's Culpable Innocence: Absurdity as Moral Insanity in *Catch 22*." *Papers on Language and Literature* 15 (1979): 290-310.

Sniderman, Stephen L. "It was all Yossarians Fault: Power and Responsibility in *Catch 22*." Nagel. 33-39.

Sorkin, Adam. "From Papa to Yo Yo at War with Words in the World". *South Atlantic Bulletin* (1979): 48-64.

Sundquist, Eric. "Naturalism in American Literature". www.wsn.com.: 4.

The Free Encyclopedia.: 2.

Trilling, Diana. "Morality and Irwin Shaw". *Midwestern Quarterly* 4 (1980): 325.

Todd, Richard. "The Marks of Kurt Vonnegut". *Conversations with Kurt Vonnegut*. Ed. William Rodney Allen. University Press Mississippi, 1988.

Uffen, Ellen Sealen. "James Jones's Trilogy, or Is War Really Hell"? *Mid America* 10 (1983): 139-51.

Viorst, Milton. "James Jones". *Contemporary Authors* 5 (1982): 253.

Volpe, Edmund. "James Jones-Norman Mailer". *Contemporary American Novelists*. Ed. Harry & Moore. Crosscurrents/ Modern Critiques. Carbondale: Southern Illinois University Press, 1964: 106-19.

Waldmeir, Joseph. "Two Novelists of the Absurd: Heller and Kesy". *Contemporary Literature V*. USA.

Waldron, Randall H. "The Naked, the Dead, and the Machine: A New Look at Mailer's First Novel." *PMLA* 87.2 (1972): 271-77.

Waugh, Patricia. "Post Modernism: Metafiction".

Way, Brian. "Formal Experiments and Social Discontent: Joseph Heller's *Catch 22*". *Journal of American Studies* 2.2 (1968): 253-70.

Wikipedia, "Firebombing of Dresden." www.wikipedia.org

Wilson, Raymond III. "Control and Freedom in the Naked and the Dead". *Texas Studies in Literature and Language* 28.2 (1986): 164-81.

Wright, Booth. "The Existential Adventure and War: Three Case Studies from American Fiction." *New Essays on American Thought and Attitude*. New York.